BUD WATSON

THE SIGMA MALE BIBLE

An Ultimate Guide To The Lone Wolf - How To Be A Sigma - Psychology Of Attraction, Dating Secrets and Strategies. Art Of Confidence, Habits & Self-Discipline. Sigma Male vs Alpha Male

First published by Halcyon Time Press 2021

Copyright © 2021 by Bud Watson

First edition

Contents

1

CHAPTER 1: THE LONE WOLF - SIGMA MALE

I n the socio-sexual hierarchy, an Alpha male is often recognized as the most dominant man in his social circles, which includes his professional and personal life as well. An Alpha male is THE one - always the center of attention, and perpetually direct, assertive, and dominant wherever he steps.

* * *

Alpha respects himself, has confidence and is not afraid to take the initiative. He is persistent, mostly aware of himself, and has high emotional intelligence, so he can always recognize when the time is right. The chances are that Alpha entices glances whenever he steps into a room, and somehow, we can recognize his dominance, even though his intentions are often non-intrusive. In the same social hierarchy, a Beta male is a loyal lieutenant to his Alpha and is there to support him and often relies on his well-rehearsed characteristics of an Alpha male.

In this dual nature of socio-sexual hierarchy, there is a male type that can "compete" with an Alpha – the mysterious lone wolf with a multitude of characteristics noted in Alphas but with a pinch of bewildering sugar and spice – the Sigma male.

The Sigma male is equally attractive as Alpha and could probably be THE Alpha if he wanted to but chooses to stay in the shadows and enjoy his own time under his conditions. Alphas often subdue to social norms that demand the man to be strong, independent, and dominant, while the Sigma male is all those things in his core but with a curious twist – Sigmas just don't care!

Are you a Sigma or looking into the world of Sigma males who often choose to go outside expected social norms? Or are you looking to become one and achieve your goals with the same ease that natural-born Sigmas do?

Sigmas are wanderers, loners, lone wolves on a mission to find themselves and enjoy life to its fullest. They are not afraid to take the initiative but don't scorn themselves when they choose not to. It is a fluid type that can find beauty in productive idleness and in the dynamics of taking action. Chosen and facultative solitude is a blessing for a Sigma male – he can grow, learn, enjoy the little things, work on professional and personal improvements, or just go with the flow and see where the solace takes him. A Sigma is as comfortable in social situations as in spending some alone time, so the possibilities are endless and many.

The lone wolf is alone only when he feels like being alone and can explore life from a different perspective, although that doesn't mean that his will can be easily shaken or that his morale is necessarily flexible – while a Sigma knows what he wants, other people usually have a hard time finding out what he wants. Hence, the mysterious aura that fits so well to the socio-sexual archetype of a Sigma male.

You can awaken the Sigma in you without the pressure of becoming an Alpha but with all social amenities that come with the archetype of the dominant male type.

INTRODUCTION INTO THE WORLD OF MYSTERIOUS SIGMA MALES

Sigmas are the new "it" guys, which seems to be already part of socio-sexual standards in contemporary times. Simply put, the Sigma male is a silent Alpha that can't seem to hide all the "alpha-ness" that he is projecting. However, he still chooses to live outside standard norms, where the social hierarchy dominant archetype Alpha exists with his "faithful" wingman Beta. Sigma is most certainly aware of traditional roles when it comes to socializing but chooses not to categorize himself as either Alpha or Beta, nor is he recognized as either of these social types.

Sigma does share a great number of qualities of an Alpha but is in a sense more introverted in expressing these characteristics, although he is equally self-confident, decisive, assertive, and even brave.

You may already be able to recognize some similarities you share with the archetype of a Sigma male; however, we are going to break down the morphology and anatomy of Sigmas to the very core of their natural attraction and "near-Zen" lifestyle.

What is a Sigma Male?

In a nutshell, the definition of a Sigma male describes this archetype as a lone wolf and a wanderer in search of his true self. In perhaps less poetic words, a Sigma male is a socio-sexual archetype with the near-same qualities of an Alpha when it comes to dominance but chooses not to conform with traditional social roles and archetypic categorization.

To create a pretext to the way males are categorized into different archetype classes, this socio-sexual hierarchy was created by the writer Theodore Robert Beale, under the name Vox Day around 2010. According to this hierarchy, males knowingly or unknowingly categorize themselves as either Alphas, Betas, or Sigmas, while Omegas and Gammas also fall into this hierarchical division.

An example of a Sigma male that may help you create a picture of how a Sigma male behaves might be one of the internet's most favorite movie celebrities – Keanu Reeves. The press often digs through Keanu's private life and ever-hungry fans, so we know that Mr. Reeves is a mindful man who chooses a solitary path and a modest, fulfilled life over fame and a lavish lifestyle. This behavior is certainly out of the social norm in the context of his financial and social possibilities, given his status and popularity. He is charming, modest, self-conscious, confident, focused on professional and personal growth, often seemingly unavailable, faithful, cares for his family and family values, and is also a rather attractive man with a unique "I don't care (but I do)" attitude – a fine picture of a Sigma male.

To stick to our example, he would have every opportunity he needs to act as an Alpha, but he chooses not to, walking a more solitary but fulfilled path.

Some of the main qualities that characterize a Sigma male are:

- Appreciation of solitude and alone time
- Flexibility of perception
- Mental strength
- Self-sufficiency
- Self-confidence
- Authenticity and uniqueness
- Natural leaders that don't impose
- Self-awareness
- Critical thinkers
- Can easily fit in but rarely do
- Decisive
- Close with only a few people
- Risk takers and brave
- Charismatic
- Independent
- Effortless attention grabber
- Rebellion
- Focus
- Appreciating the present moment
- Non-judgmental

When talking about an archetypical behavior of a Sigma male, we can say that Sigmas are often other people's favorites, which includes a great potential to be favored by Alphas as well; however, not many people can say that they are a Sigma's favorite. While Sigmas are attractive and mysterious, in part for having ambiguous morale and being non-judgmental, Sigmas choose to live outside social norms and are rarely close to a great number of people. Many Sigmas don't have a close friend or have limited their social circle to a single best friend or two buddies.

A Sigma never relies on other people and rather lives off the grid, searching for his path where he works on fulfilling his goals, exploring the world and life itself, or just enjoys living in the moment. Thus, social challenges that may include competing with Alphas and Betas are of no concern or interest to Sigmas, which adds to their unavailability – another attractive trait noted in Sigmas.

He doesn't care about the hierarchy sometimes out of silent rebellion and, at times, just because he doesn't care – a Sigma doesn't need gratification from others to take action and is self-sufficient in the sense of the motivation behind his actions and initiatives.

Just as anyone can transform into an Alpha or a Beta, a status of a Sigma male is also achievable with another trait that Sigma's have – the will for self-improvement. Before you start working on becoming a Sigma male or improving your "sigma-ness," let's see some of the main differences and similarities between Alphas and Sigmas.

Alpha Male vs. Sigma Male

Sigmas, much like Alphas, are decisive, attractive, and interesting within their respective social circles and are both natural leaders. Like Alphas, a Sigma male can fit into most social circles and can be well-accepted by everyone. Other similarities between Alphas and Sigmas are self-confidence, self-respect, mental strength, and focus. The ability to attract other people is also a shared trait between the two hierarchical etiquettes.

Therefore, if Alphas and Sigmas are so similar, what makes them different, and what are the core traits that set these two types apart?

Even though both Alphas and Sigmas are natural leaders, Alphas naturally pursue a role of leadership, while Sigmas don't care about leading or imposing their leadership on anyone. Whether you like or don't like a Sigma, it doesn't make any difference to him. If a Sigma appreciates himself and his own company, there aren't many things in the world that can make them lose that balance.

Alphas can fit anywhere and are often respected and likable across a multitude of different social groups, which flatters their character and motivates them to "stay at the top of their game." On the other hand, Sigmas can fit into any social situation or group, but they often choose not to fit in and don't feel comfortable with everyone. They likely keep their social circles narrow and limited to a few people at best. Their trust is hard to earn at times, and they would not share things with many people.

Along with the self-confidence of a Sigma is self-respect and self-awareness, which means that Sigmas are often aware of their flaws, as well as their traits. They don't try to be liked by everyone, which is the opposite case with Alphas. Alpha males can employ social tactics to fit in and get accepted as "in charge," i.e., as an Alpha of the group. Alphas are often dominant and won't accept the possibility of letting someone else take their spotlight. Alphas have a lot of expectations from other people that they feel the need to fulfill, such as always being the best version of yourself – always being dominant – whereas Sigmas don't feel that kind of pressure. They live under their conditions and are set to fulfill only those expectations that they have for themselves. Not caring about what others think is one of the major differences between Alphas and Sigmas, and guess which of the two doesn't care at all!

Alphas may often use other males, Betas, to show off their qualities in the best light possible and will compare Betas to themselves, indirectly or directly, mostly in scenarios that involve women and flirting. On the contrary, Sigma doesn't need to show his dominance to others to stand out from the crowd and attract some interest – the lonely wolf trope seems to be working just fine for a Sigma.

Moreover, while Alphas are dependent in the sense of social acceptance and gratification received from others to feel like an Alpha and be THE Alpha, Sigmas are independent and would rather choose off the grid, "nomadic" lives. Alphas can truly be Alphas in specific conditions, where they can show their dominance and where they can be heard and seen. In that sense, Alphas can be described as somewhat extreme extraverts that feed off the attention they get. Sigmas would rather stay out of this case scenario and choose silence as one of their strongest attributes. Sigma doesn't do anything in exchange for gratification or appreciation, while he appreciates silence as much as Alphas appreciate dynamic social environments.

Since Alphas depend on acceptance and gratification, as well as being in charge, they often don't perform well in groups where they are not THE leaders. More ambitious Alphas may see everyone as a threat or competition or as Betas, professionally or personally. Quite the opposite, Sigmas function perfectly well in groups and alone, as they appreciate constructive solitude. While they don't observe others as competitors, a Sigma "grades" people by their sets of value and how well they get along over how much "better or worse" someone is in comparison to themselves.

The need to belong in a certain environment that brings out the leader in them is very much present in the Alpha's world – social acceptance, gratification, and appreciation are the fuel of Alphas. Sigmas don't require that form of validation, which is why the need to belong barely exists or doesn't exist at all – Sigmas are quite self-sufficient in that sense as well.

The constant need for Alphas to reinsert their dominance and show everyone that they are "the leaders of the pack" may at times be seen as repulsive in other people's perception. That need also erases almost any sign of humility that may exist in an Alpha male. Bragging, competitiveness, and intrusive ambition may often be "side effects" of siding with Alphas.In the same matter, Sigmas have a higher level of humility as they tend to keep their achievements to themselves – they don't need other people to know that they are good or the best at something to feel good about themselves.

If we summed up the main difference between Alphas and Sigmas, this differentiating factor would be social pressure or the lack of it in the case of a Sigma male. While Alpha may be in constant fear of losing his position as a dominant individual, feeling the pressure of staying at the top, Sigmas don't feel the pressure of social validation and acceptance. Sigmas may be perceived as mysterious and even introverted because of this, but they rarely care how others perceive them, which relieves the pressure of being accepted. That leaves Sigmas with living the life they want and being who they are.

The Silent Superiority and Attraction of Sigma Males

Where an Alpha would rely on social circles to attract and meet women, often an extrovert, Sigmas rather use a cold approach by being what they are – mysterious, intriguing, and seemingly unapproachable, which makes them extremely attractive to women. Alpha may use other people in his surroundings to show his superiority and attract a potential partner, while Sigmas will often rely on themselves and on traits they have to offer in such situations.

Are women more likely to choose a Sigma male over Alpha?

Not always, and it greatly depends on different preferences – some women prefer Alpha males and appreciate the dominant type it represents, while others may be hooked to the intrigue of the mysterious Sigma male who doesn't talk too much but tells a lot with silence and a few words.

But why do women find Sigmas attractive?

To break down the silent superiority and attraction that many women have for Sigma males, Sigma males will rarely fully give themselves to a girl, or almost anyone for that matter. This can make the girl in question hooked on always wanting more – wanting to find out more about the Sigma to get close to him and win his affection – in a nutshell, Sigma poses as someone hard to get.

Playing "hard to get" comes naturally to Sigmas, as they don't make themselves unapproachable with the intention to manipulate someone – that is just their characteristic. However, this trait can be learned and implemented, even if it doesn't feel natural. Many Sigmas have rusty social skills, which is why we can't say that a Sigma would manipulate someone into liking them or going after them romantically.

Another trait that makes Sigmas irresistible is their independence. Women like independent men who work on their goals and know what they want and how to get it. Independence can even be called the "new sexy," as assertiveness and taking action means that you are trying and doing your best to get where you want in life. Sigmas don't wait for others to tell them how to grab their opportunities, chase their dreams and fulfill their goals – they take action and rely on themselves, which is more than just a sexy trait. Sigmas accept their responsibilities and are not afraid to face the consequences of failure. However, in this case, the most important of all is that Sigmas know how to recover and get up when they are down. Quitting is not an option for a true Sigma.

Many people, including Alphas, will fabricate their public and social personality to attract other people and make girls like them. They also construct a well-worked-out ego to hide all the negative traits they might be aware of. Sigmas are less likely to hide negative characteristics as they can learn to improve themselves and accept themselves for who they are, which is why Sigmas usually feel comfortable in their skin. This case reflects self-confidence, self-acceptance, and self-improvement goals, which are likewise attractive to other people. Honesty to oneself and others is an important aspect of becoming a true Sigma male.

An Alpha male is more likely to calculate the risk of approaching a girl they like as there is a fear of acting as a Beta in case someone rejects them. If a girl rejects an ambitious and confident Alpha, he is also more likely to ask for social gratification and validation elsewhere to feel like Alpha again. A Sigma knows how to accept rejection and respect different choices. They rarely impose themselves, which is yet another attractive quality that may get Sigma a date.

What Sigma knows is that every rejection is a new opportunity to work on yourself and find out what you are doing wrong.

When a Sigma enters the room where there is an Alpha male in all the glory of alpha-ness, women are more likely to first notice the extrovert and often attention-seeking Alpha. However, as the evening unravels, seeing a Sigma comfortably sitting by himself and glancing over at a girl he is interested in can even make the girl decide to approach and start talking to a Sigma - a mysterious and silent guy open for an honest conversation. Attractive, right?

A Sigma doesn't have to be physically attractive to be interesting to women, as his traits and characteristics can compensate for the lack of physical attraction – the "whatever" attitude, mystery and intrigue, freedom, ambiguity, and tasteful rebellion is what gives off the "bad boy vibes" that many girls find attractive. What they are getting is an honest man, a good listener but a catch hard to get and approach.

The fact that Sigmas don't comply with the standard and traditional socio-sexual roles and dominance hierarchy amplifies their attractiveness. They also refuse to conform with the dominance hierarchy when they could obviously be Alphas, but they rebel against formal expectations that other people have for them. They are more likely to dress extravagantly or have a unique style, while a lifestyle of a Sigma is often different from what is expected. Different means unexplored, and unexplored entices more interest and can make the girl you like wonder if you can like her the way she likes you. What is he thinking? What does he like? What is he like? All these questions are the product of the aura of mystery that Sigmas reflect that can help them win the girl and attract other people.

BETA MALE QUALITIES THAT WORK AGAINST YOU

Betas are usually known as faithful wingmen and good lieutenants whose role is to support the Alpha in their social circle, but being a Beta is more complex than just being Alpha's support.

Betas are not unattractive or unable to be the leaders; they just like to play safe and often go for less risky choices compared to Alphas and Sigmas. According to the socio-sexual hierarchy, most men are Betas, defined as the faithful followers of Alphas. Betas are described as men who rarely have their vision and philosophy and are more likely to rely on others to tell them what to do. However, being a Beta is not bad – far from it – if you are Beta, you are fierce in your own way, loyal and a good friend to others, always there for people who need your help and can recognize the value of leadership. This can make them successful and attractive, even in a room with an Alpha and Sigma.

Even though Betas are open, friendly, supportive, hard-working, and respect others, Betas have some negative traits that they may share with other archetypes, like Alphas and Sigmas. The lack of confidence and lack of action are some of the Beta male qualities that may work against you and that you may recognize among your traits and characteristics. Here are some of the main qualities characteristic of Betas that may get in your way of becoming a true Sigma.

The Lack of Self-Confidence

One of the most important traits that separate Alphas and Sigmas from Betas is self-confidence. Many Betas have what it takes to either be an Alpha or a Sigma but lack the confidence needed to embrace a different archetype in the social hierarchy, so they choose to stay in the back alley and leave things as they are. There is nothing wrong with being a Beta or choosing to rely on others for support = after all, Alphas rely on Betas in a way. However, when it comes to the lack of self-confidence, this case may push you towards relying on others for important decision-making.

Betas are often afraid of the consequences of their choices, so they would rather let others choose on their behalf, which can lead to missed opportunities and unfulfilled potential in their professional and personal life. The lack of self-confidence may surely keep you stranded on your way towards becoming a Sigma but don't worry, we got you covered, as you will learn how to retrieve your self-confidence and how to trust your own choices by the end of this guide.

The Lack of Action

With the lack of self-confidence, there is a lack of action just around the corner. It is difficult to act when you don't trust your own choices and don't think you are good enough or believe in your qualities. Many Betas just decide to go with the flow, hoping everything will resolve itself – some things can resolve by themselves, but many call for action. People who take action and seize every opportunity that comes their way are more likely to achieve their goals and live the life they want, not the life that others want them to live. Unfortunately, the lack of self-confidence may restrain your progress in life as you are less likely to act even on opportunities that appear once in a lifetime that are perfect for you.

This lack of action and idleness can affect your personal and professional life and prevent you from exploring life and becoming the best version of yourself. To resolve this problem, you need to get rid of the fear you might be hiding within. We will teach you how to become a man of action as you progress through our guide.

Misguided Attraction

Betas are often "victims" to misguided attraction, which means that some Betas may have a hard time reading the signs when it comes to being romantically interested in someone. A great number of insecurities and a lack of self-confidence may make a Beta feel like he doesn't stand a chance with a girl he likes, being misguided and often having poor social skills to communicate and let other people know what he exactly wants. On the other hand, Betas are also often emotionally available and can communicate their emotions openly; however, this may backfire when they are not sure how to read other people's emotions. That may lead Betas to either think they have a strong chance with someone they don't, or that they don't stand a chance with a person who actually shares their feelings. Misguided attraction is the side effect of the lack of self-confidence, fear, insecurities, and often poor communication skills. As you move on to the following chapters, you will learn how to trust yourself, read other people's emotions and body language, and attract the good things you want in your life.

Self-criticism

Being self-aware is one of the greatest traits of Sigmas, as Sigmas are usually very much familiar with their character qualities, the flaws and traits alike. On the other hand, this awareness may easily turn into self-criticism and vice versa. Betas usually have many insecurities, which prevents them from being more dominant and more extroverted in expressing their otherwise interesting personalities. Recognizing your shortcomings and flaws is a good thing, as this means that you can improve yourself and become a better person for your good and for the sake of achieving your goals more easily. However, there is a fine line between self-criticism and self-awareness, which can lead to more insecurities and cause a lack of self-confidence, a lack of action, and some personality issues that can make you doubt yourself. We are all flawed, and we all have our qualities; what makes a difference is working on improving yourself.

Before you learn how to stop criticizing yourself for every little thing that goes bad, you need to learn to love and respect yourself. Luckily, we have you covered in the upcoming chapters of our guide on How to Become a Sigma.

The Need to Please People

Betas are usually defined as genuine people pleasers. They are assertive when it comes to making other people feel good about themselves, which is an extraordinary trait as long as they don't forget to please themselves. Many Betas often put themselves in plan B and take care of other people's needs before their own. Prioritizing everyone else's needs over yours is not a problem until it starts consuming your life and you realize that every action you have taken in your life was for someone else's good or pleasure. What about yourself? What about the things you want and need?

You need to realize that you are not being selfish if you say "No" when you feel like saying NO. Being a Yes Man is a good thing when it comes to seizing the day and achieving your goals, but if you depend on pleasing others and forget about your own needs, it will harm you in the long run. It is perfectly fine to go an extra mile for people you love and appreciate and who love you and respect you back, but pleasing everyone at all times will take more of the energy you need to become what you want to be. Take care not to get used and abused by other people, as sometimes others can sense your inability to say NO and your need to please others. Some people may exploit you for it, which is why you build up your insecurities and forget about your own needs and wants. Remember, you are not selfish if you say NO when you feel like it.

Submissive Behavior

According to the dominance hierarchy, Betas are followers, and Alphas are leaders. In this case scenario, Sigmas have everything it takes to become a leader but has no interest in being one. The difference here between a Sigma and a Beta male is that Sigma has a choice not to be the Alpha, and Beta chooses to follow a suitable leadership model, which takes the Beta to submissive behavior. Betas may often be agreeable with their model of leadership and show a lack of decisiveness and assertiveness, even when they don't agree with something.

Betas may also depend on social validation, primarily seeking acceptance from Alphas, which can make them feel better about themselves. Thus, the first sign that you are far from becoming a Sigma is the need to follow other people and the very need for acceptance, gratification, and validation from others. Once you learn how to appreciate yourself and recognize your true needs, you will get rid of the signs of submissive behavior and learn how to become a leader and not a follower.

THE TRUE VIRTUES OF SIGMA MALES

What may be more attractive than a loud and confident leader is a person that has all the qualities of a leader and can easily become one but just doesn't want to. This would be a Sigma male. Sigmas have a multitude of virtues that make them attractive to other people, while they don't even try to please others or tailor their personalities so that other people appreciate them.

Sigmas don't conform unless they are comfortable and never feel the need to compensate for their nonconformity when it comes to other people. They just don't see any value in being bound by other people's expectations and norms. Such character leaves a lot of space for personal and professional growth, as Sigmas are often silent leaders and even innovators, following their capacities. A true Sigma will always allow themselves to fulfill their potential and live up to their expectations. We will break down all the virtues and qualities in detail that make a Sigma what he is - a lone wolf who doesn't

THE SIGMA MALE BIBLE

conform and is comfortable in his skin.

Tasteful Rebellion

Sigmas can often be perceived as reckless because they choose to do what they want and not what other people want them to do. They rebel against traditional roles in the social hierarchy and the generally established norms. The tasteful rebellion is attractive to many people and ladies alike, which, in part, is why Sigmas are so appealing to others, even if they don't try to suit everyone's taste. There is a strange attraction in nonconformity and silent rebellion that seems to place a Sigma male on the top of the hierarchy, yet, he refuses to be a part of it. Rebellion is most certainly one of the most attractive traits that make Sigma what he is; however, that doesn't mean that everyone who refuses to get along with norms is a Sigma. A Sigma is not a criminogenic person that refuses to comply with the law; he just doesn't conform with standard social norms that come with certain expectations – go to college, find an office job that pays well, buy a house, get married, start a family, retire and enjoy the remaining years of your life. This timeline of expectations usually doesn't sound appealing to Sigmas, who are often seen for alternatives that can grant them some sort of freedom and the opportunity to manage their time under their conditions.

Uniqueness

Sigma males often have a unique sense of fashion and know how to attract people's interest at first sight, as well as keeping them engaged with their personalities in the long run, almost effortlessly. Not many Sigmas are extravagant, but they are certainly unique in the way they express themselves. More often, the way they dress and groom reflects their non-conformity, although not many Sigmas are eccentric but most do stand out from the crowd. This uniqueness is not only seen in their physical appearance and their style but is also noted in their personality. Sigma is less likely to follow the well-established norm of working in an office from nine to five after graduating college, and he is less likely to choose companionship over his freedom.

The freedom of choice is very important to Sigmas, as they like their wings spread wide and ready to take flight whenever they feel like it. This may characterize Sigmas as somewhat volatile in other people's perception, but this is just how Sigmas are – unapologetically free. If someone were to date a Sigma, they would have a hard time controlling his "outbursts of freedom" and keeping that Sigma by their side. Sigmas don't like to be constrained and don't appreciate anyone trying to control what they do and how they act. Their choices are their own, and even though these choices may appear impulsive at times, Sigmas are collected and place major value on critical thinking and logic.

Unavailability

Unavailability or the fact that Sigmas seem difficult to approach and grab their attention is one of the key characteristics other people find attractive in a Sigma male. "Playing hard to get" comes naturally to a Sigma and is far from being a form of intentional manipulation. Instead, a Sigma is busy with his own goals and interests, which takes most of his time and focus, also unintentionally creating an aura of mystery and intrigue. This mystery and intrigue are what captures people's attention. By showing people that you value your own time and space and that you would appreciate it if others would value it, too, you are setting your availability and the lack of it to your terms and standards. This quality is appealing to many people who are attracted to the virtues of Sigmas.

Going deeper into the psychology of this feeling, we can't seem to miss that a great number of people enjoy pursuing challenges like capturing the interest of a Sigma male. It may be difficult to capture Sigma's attention to its fullest extent because Sigma doesn't need other people's attention to thrive. This is also why people feel special when they manage to attract someone whose attention is hard to get and who seems to be impossible to impress but worthy of impressing - it's hard to achieve and thus rewarding once you do.

Mindfulness

Entering the state of mindfulness is not an easy task – it takes some time and some discipline and dedication but is certainly worth all the time invested. To define mindfulness, we can say that it is a state of being present in the moment or the ability to be fully present. Mindfulness also means being fully over the present events and all the sensations these experiences involve without having an explosive or radical reaction to what is going on. It is the ability to be present and stay open-minded as you use critical thinking and logic to experience different situations in life.

Sigma is known as a mindful type that can enjoy the present to its fullest and utilize every opportunity he gets. To fully appreciate life and its endless possibilities while following your dreams is how most Sigmas "operate." Mindfulness help Sigmas focus on their goals while allowing them to enjoy alone time and work on self-improvements, making it one of the key virtues noted in most Sigmas.

Mindfulness is also practical, as it reduces stress levels, anxieties and can increase awareness so you can focus on important things in your life, as well the things you lack so you can pursue them. Mindfulness can be practiced and learned, and you will have a chance to tackle some of the 101 basics of practicing and mastering mindfulness further in our guide.

Self-consciousness

Sigmas are self-conscious, as we have already pointed out earlier in the book. This characteristic helps Sigmas be aware of their traits, as well as their shortcomings and negative characteristics. Of course, nobody is perfect, but Sigmas are surely trying to live up to their expectations by working on self-improvement. Without self-consciousness and being fully aware of your personality traits, improvement wouldn't be possible.

According to ancient Greek philosophers, one of the biggest tasks in one's life is to know yourself. "Know Yourself" was also written on some of the preserved Delphi temples, where ancient Greeks would come for answers about their lives, future, and the meaning of life. Today, knowing yourself still poses a difficult task, as we often empathize with ourselves, which is more than normal. You can feel other people's pain, and you can see other people through your perception, but you will always feel your pain and emotions the most, above other people's emotions. This is where the self-consciousness starts −realizing your potential and the possibilities you carry through your personality traits. Being self-conscious also allows you to become what you want to be, as you can see what part of your personality should be worked on and improved to achieve your goals.

Respect and Self-respect

A Sigma respects himself, but he also respects other people – even though Sigmas may lack relationships in life and may have a hard time sticking around in other people's lives, they respect other people's privacy, wants, needs, and philosophies. This allows Sigmas to be nonjudgmental – it's very easy for Sigmas to accept the fact that we are all different and perhaps quirky in our way, so they can get along with practically anyone if they are motivated to socialize.

By respecting yourself, you acknowledge your personality traits as a part of you that makes you who you are. That also means that you value your time and that you won't settle down for anything for the sake of pleasing others. Self-respect doesn't mean that Sigma is placing himself above everyone else. It rather means that Sigma is very much aware that we all have the same rights, regardless of the differences in character, skill set, personality, social class, and other determining factors.

If you are struggling with respecting yourself and others, and you are aware that there is a problem with self-respect, we got you covered as you will be able to practice self-respect with a lesson that awaits you in the following chapters.

Easily Adaptable

A great understanding of other people's motifs, body language, and behavior allows a Sigma to be easily adaptable to any situation that may come his way. This is a rather handy trait in professional and personal life, as Sigmas can find their way in any social situation and give their best performance at work, that way making progress in life.

However, Sigma is less likely to adapt to situations and experiences he is not comfortable with, as Sigmas are anything but conformists. Sigmas pursue their happiness in life by doing what they like and how they like, making them independent and brave. Adapting to various situations is an amazing social and life skill, but Sigmas usually choose not to adapt as they appreciate living their life under their own terms. However, that doesn't mean that a Sigma can't choose to adapt if he wants to – he has the potential but usually prefers not to conform. The case is similar to being an Alpha, as Sigma has all the potential to become an Alpha but rather chooses to stay out of the social hierarchy of dominance.

A Man of Few Words

A Sigma is a man of few words. If he doesn't have anything to say that would provide value to a conversation, a Sigma would rather stay silent. While Alphas and Betas may be involved in mundane talks that usually don't take the conversation anywhere new, Sigmas carefully choose their words and only speak if they consider they have something clever to say. If you are a true Sigma, there is no need for unnecessary and unmeaningful dialogue.

This provides Sigma with a reputation of a rational man and a critical thinker. At the same time, he is also considered to be even more mysterious and intriguing as he doesn't talk too much, thus not revealing much about himself either. Unlike Alphas that like to point out their virtues and positive traits, Sigmas will never talk about themselves from that perspective.

Now that you have learned everything there is to know about Sigma personality, and you know more about the differences and similarities between different socio-sexual types according to the Vox Day hierarchy, you can move forward to important lessons and practices that should help you learn everything about being a Sigma and ultimately assist you in becoming a Sigma male.

2

CHAPTER 2: SIGMA MIND, SIGMA VIBES

The words "positive mind, positive vibes" are so deeply ingrained into modern culture that this maxim has somewhat become a cliché. But what is interesting about clichés is that these usually carry truthful and honest messages that have become frequently repeated for a good reason. We can apply a similar philosophy to our goal of becoming a Sigma male, as all changes first start from your mind.

We are beings of energy, fueled not only by food and water but with good (positive) and bad (negative) energy. Positive thinking comes with many benefits, stress reduction, reduced risk of illness and depression, better coping mechanisms and fear-free life, and ultimately more quality life. The chances are that many things that are not going well for you are induced through negative thoughts and destructive negative thinking, which can easily become a never-ending cycle of despair if you don't identify it as a negative thing that it represents.

Identifying negative thoughts is sometimes not as easy and simple as it sounds. Some people might have trouble differentiating negative thoughts for realistic thoughts based on pure logic. This is often the case with people who have been stuck for too long in the cycle of negative thinking to the point where it transforms into self-sabotage.

The change starts with your decision to recognize the negative patterns and implement a healthier way of thinking. Overlooking the good things in life and focusing on the bad experiences is one of the "side effects" of negative thinking, which further attracts negative energy in your life that you can also project onto other people. Imagine that you had a great time with your friends yesterday – you had some drinks, you talked to a pretty girl, or you just had a promotion and wanted to celebrate – suddenly, as you are on your way home, it starts to rain, and you get soaking wet and splashed on by speeding cars. You can choose to remember this night by the great time you had before the rain, or you can wallow in negativity and remember the bad things, i.e., the rain that you couldn't control that caught you by surprise.

You can learn to remain positive even in frustrating situations by "cleansing" your thoughts and identifying negativity that affects your life and your decisions. You can't let things that you can't control affect the rest of your day or the rest of your week if it makes you feel bad about yourself. It's the same case with learning how to become a Sigma. "Sigma mind, Sigma vibes" should capture the idea of this chapter in a nutshell, as you will learn how to think like a Sigma to become one.

The first step towards your transformation is to accept yourself, respect yourself, and learn how to appreciate yourself, so you can recreate yourself and become what you want to be.

Building self-confidence and self-esteem are steps you will go through towards reinventing yourself into a true Sigma, along with learning how to appreciate and trust yourself, how to grow, and how to build and achieve your goals.

ACCEPT YOURSELF, RECREATE YOURSELF

The first step towards a genuine change is to accept yourself. After you accept yourself with all the virtues and flaws and learn how to appreciate yourself for who you are and who you want to become, will you be able to truly reinvent yourself and recreate your life to fit your goals, needs, and wants?

The first step is also the hardest step on your journey to becoming a Sigma.

To accept yourself, you need to be honest with yourself, and while honesty may not be a problem for you, it may be difficult to stay completely objective when it comes to being honest about yourself. Analyze everything about yourself – your goals, needs, achievements, things you are proud of about yourself, and those things you are not happy about. Write down everything on paper or on your laptop in a separate document so you can have a clear and objective insight into everything you like about your life and those things you want to change and implement new "traditions."

To help you with the hardest step of all, we break down the road to acceptance into smaller goals that you can gradually work on towards your achievement once you accept yourself. You will combine these steps and work on them daily by dealing with smaller, easily achievable goals, one by one. By combining these steps for acceptance and the following practices in this chapter, you should be able to recreate yourself into the true Sigma that you want to become.

Step 1: Objective Perception

Objectivity is the key factor for identifying your character traits in the light of logic and reality. Being objective with people we love or appreciate is sometimes difficult enough, so being in your skin, it is even more difficult to objectively evaluate yourself. However, objectivity is vital in the process of acceptance. Be objective and list your virtues and flaws, your achievements, and your failures. List all the improvements you want to work on, so you can start accepting yourself for who you are.

Step 2: Be Honest

Be honest with yourself and other people. Honesty will take you a long way, and you will even feel better, perhaps after you feel a bit worse, because truth can be painful at times. To deal with the pain, you have already embraced the reality of things in the first step, and you know what you are facing and what needs to be dealt with. Be honest about all the things you would change about yourself and all the things you appreciate about yourself.

Step 3: Accept Responsibility

Even in experiences that we can't control, we still retain a portion of sovereignty over these situations in how we react to them. To get back to the story of negativity and positivity, we can't control the rain that caught us by surprise, but we can control our reaction to the rain, and we may decide whether we put that unpleasant experience behind us or just move on and focus on things that matter. Take responsibility for your life, even when it is not your fault that something bad happened. Take responsibility for choices that got you where you are in the present, for better or for worse. By taking responsibility for our actions and choices, we also regain control over our lives.

Step 4: Admit When You Are Wrong

Nobody is right all the time, and that is a fact. Admitting when you are wrong can relieve you of the great burden of having to deal with an avalanche of regrets for not accepting responsibility for your actions. This is a major step, as it can be difficult to admit to ourselves that we have wronged. Nobody is perfect, and we all make mistakes, which is a perfectly normal thing. What is important is to know how to handle the situation when you have made a mistake, which is to get the best out of the worst possible case scenarios.

The easiest way to admit that you were wrong and move on is to perceive your faults as new learning opportunities and as a way to grow and improve yourself. This way, you can find the strength within you to shape your own life and accept reality as it is.

Step 5: Be Aware of Your Strengths

The road to acceptance is now just admitting that you were wrong and accepting your negative traits and things in life that you want to improve. You need to be aware of your strengths and virtues and all those things you like about yourself that don't need changing. Your strengths will be the spinning wheel behind your transformation. List all your strengths and plan on how you can utilize them smartly to achieve your goals.

Step 6: No Fear Allowed

Fear and anxieties are your biggest enemies on the way to accepting yourself and becoming who you want to be. Often, we sabotage ourselves with self-inducing fears, negative thinking and a lack of self-confidence. At the same time, many of us also listen to other people who project their fears onto us. Fear can paralyze you and prevent you from embracing positive thinking and inviting positive changes into your life. So, what is the worst thing that can happen? The worst thing might be to fail, but if you view failure as a learning curve, you will have no fear about the future, and you will be truly free.

Step 7: Struggles Are a Normal Part of Reality

All people have struggles; even those who seem the happiest encounter troubles in life. Life is filled with beauty but is also full of challenges that can shape you and form your personality. You are the one who chooses how your personality will change following your actions and reactions. There will always be a struggle, as it is a perfectly natural component of life that can serve the purpose of pushing your personal growth. Smartly utilize struggles by turning every bump on the road into a valuable life lesson that can take you closer to your goals and help you accept reality without being biased.

Step 8: Focus on Your Goals

List your goals and think through how you can change and work on yourself to achieve your goals. You can work on smaller goals and achievements each day as you are working towards completing major goals, which should give you the needed self-confidence daily. For example, if you want to become more fit, you can't achieve your goal at once. You can break down the main goal into smaller tasks that will help you achieve becoming more fit. Create a routine and a plan for your workouts and work on it every day to stay disciplined. Each day is a small new success that you build up daily towards achieving a major goal. You can apply micro-tasking to almost any goal you have. The most important thing is to remain dedicated and focused on your goals and the best way to reach them.

To accept yourself and recreate yourself, you also need to practice self-love and self-esteem, so let's see the best way to reinstate these two qualities.

Practicing Self-love

How to love yourself? Well, how do you love anyone, for that matter? We love people even beyond imperfections, sometimes because we see them through our perception with a filter of improvement, and sometimes we accept all their flaws and love them anyway. The same thing goes with loving yourself

– you can pretend you are an imperfect perfection and appreciate yourself as you are without the need to change, or you can learn to love yourself despite the flaws you can recognize and work on changing everything you believe should be changed for the sake of a better life.

To practice self-love, you first need to stop comparing yourself to other people. Comparing ourselves with other people we know and meet is a perfectly normal thing; however, this is not a good thing, as it increases self-loathing and unrealistic expectations. You don't want to be like others; you want to be yourself. Therefore, you need to focus on your own goals and needs and work on achieving them regardless of other people's success or lack of it. This is another virtue of Sigmas – they are perfectly aware of people around them and all their qualities, but they are likewise aware of themselves and their own goals.

Let's see some of the commandments of self-love so you can practice appreciation for yourself and remind yourself that you deserve to be loved and appreciated.

• Don't Mind Other People's Opinion

A Sigma doesn't mind the restraints and expectations of society and what other people think of him. It is important to acknowledge and accept the opinion of people that care for you and know you very well, but considering everyone's opinion is impossible, as you can't make everyone happy. Whatever you do, there's always someone who will not appreciate the way you lead your life, so don't try to please everyone – please yourself and satisfy your vision of yourself and who you want to become. Think about what is best for you, whatever you do, over considering the expectations that others may have for you.

• Your Looks Match Your Inner State

It's not all about the looks, and you should avoid pursuing traditional beauty standards as this may hurt your self-esteem and set unrealistic expectations.

However, looks do matter when it comes to your health and the way you feel about yourself. So, work out, eat healthily and take care of your body and hygiene to look good and feel even better. More often, the way we look outside reflects how we feel on the inside, and we are sending a silent message to other people. Moreover, you can also feel better the better you look, so this bond is covalent in a way. Wear the clothes you feel comfortable and happy in, take care of your health and body, but remember that the way you look doesn't affect your inner value.

• Get Rid of Toxicity

A Sigma is an independent person who doesn't share his time with toxic people and likes to stay away from people who don't get him and try to control how they live their lives. This is a perfect example of getting rid of toxicity that comes from external factors, i.e., from people who don't mind their business. Distance yourself from toxic people who bring you down and also try to identify the toxicity coming from your thoughts. Negative thoughts are toxic, can bring us down, and have no use in our personal growth and development. There is no room for toxic behavior and toxic thoughts on your road to a true change and transformation, as this toxicity will prevent you from appreciating and loving yourself.

• Don't Wallow in Doubts

Doubt is a major obstacle in building self-love and self-esteem, as we can't trust ourselves to make a good decision if we wallow in doubt. Doubting yourself may keep you far from making progress and make you miss out on important things and great opportunities in life. You know who you are and what you are capable of – the only thing left is to trust yourself with all your potential. Even if your last decision wasn't the right one, have faith that you can make things better. Learn from the past instead of regretting it – this is the only constructive way of perceiving your reality.

- **Work on Achievements**

Achieving something, even the smallest of goals and dreams, can make us feel better about ourselves and even make us proud of ourselves. Working on achievements is an important part of your journey, as this is a great way of inserting positive change into your life while working on achievements is also a fantastic way of practicing self-love. It will be easier for you to appreciate who you are if you work on achieving your goals. All the little victories are significant if you work hard on making it.

- **You Are Your Number One**

There is nothing wrong with thinking about your well-being over other people's needs. Some people may perceive it as selfishness, but we are talking about selflessness to ourselves. It is perfectly all right to put yourself first sometimes and don't think about being selfish because of it. However, if you are always postponing putting yourself first, you will always prioritize other people's needs and wants, and it will never be your turn to work on improving yourself or just enjoying some alone time. Sigmas may be perceived as selfish, as they prioritize their alone time and the time they get to have only for themselves, but this is the right way to go if you want to become a true Sigma and learn how to love yourself.

- **Be Bold, Be Brave**

A Sigma is brave and bold – he is not afraid of speaking his mind and doesn't fear being himself in public. You need to realize that your words matter just like anyone else's, so don't be afraid to make the first move, approach a group of people or take a seat at the table without being called to join. Consider yourself welcome anywhere and everywhere and practice your boldness. Start by speaking your mind and expressing yourself – some people will like you for it, and others won't, but you know that not everyone can like you, which is a sign that you are doing quite well.

- **Don't Be Mean to Yourself**

It is easy and equally painful to indulge yourself in self-criticism when you have done something wrong or failed in something. What is more difficult and more useful for personal growth in reciprocity is to be kind to yourself, even when you feel you don't deserve kindness. The world is a place of beauty but also a universe of harsh words and criticism, so the last thing you need is to add up to all the negativities. Be at peace with yourself regardless of the situation, and you will be able to love yourself.

Practicing Self-esteem

Self-esteem is the measure of how you place value in yourself and how you respect yourself. Self-esteem is an ability to believe in yourself and, in a way, convince yourself that you can achieve anything you set your mind to. Self-esteem is not directly related to your potential or ability to do something, as you can be good at something and still have poor self-esteem, preventing you from improving your abilities or expressing yourself. In contrast, people with high self-esteem may not be as good at something but still try and perform the task due to their conviction of capability.

People with low self-esteem generally struggle with expressing themselves and believing in their ability to do something good, which is why it is rather important to work on rebuilding your self-esteem. By practicing self-esteem, you open the doors of endless possibilities, where you can do anything you want. Even if you fail, it doesn't matter since you tried. Trying is what counts in the end.

People with self-esteem don't have unrealistic expectations but have a more positive outlook on the world and a more positive perception of their place in that world, which is why it is easier for them to succeed and achieve their goals and dreams. A true Sigma has self-esteem and knows his capabilities, but he also knows that the sky is the limit if you set your mind to something. A Sigma is willing to try and is also capable of using failure as a lesson.

If you are struggling with self-esteem, follow these steps to practice retrieving faith and trust in yourself.

Step 1: Look Good, Feel Good

Sometimes, the very fact that we look good makes us feel good about ourselves. Even if you don't feel your best, try cheering yourself up by wearing your favorite outfit or adding a new shirt to your wardrobe that you can take on a walk. Looking good will feel good and will help you build your self-esteem. Whenever you feel like you are having trouble with self-esteem, put on some nice clothes or wear something that makes you feel good about yourself. This is an excellent practice for building self-esteem as it is as easy and simple as putting some nice and comfy clothes on.

Step 2: It's Not All About the Looks

To be able to fully appreciate yourself and build your self-esteem, you need to practice loving yourself, even when you don't feel good and when you don't think you look good. This step is directly related to accepting yourself the way you are and appreciating yourself for who you are and who you want to become. It's not all about the looks, that's for sure, but you will feel better if you treat yourself with love and care. That's why it's important to sometimes treat yourself, eat healthily, think positively, be active and enjoy your free time. Many things can cheer you up on a rough day, and one of these things is accepting that there is a new day ahead with new opportunities, even when you don't feel good. Your self-esteem will benefit if you go easy on yourself.

Step 3: Celebrate All Your Victories

Even the smallest of victories can become a way of achieving greatness, so every win you make should be celebrated just as a major achievement. The easiest way to achieve your goals is to complete smaller goals that you can set for yourself. Each of these small victories is a step closer to what you want and need, so there is no harm in patting your own back whenever you complete a small goal. This way, you are also practicing self-esteem as your approval will help your confidence on the road to becoming more independent and opposing external factors that can compromise your self-esteem.

Step 4: Say NO to Negativity

Negative thoughts and negative people are some of the biggest foes when it comes to tarnishing your self-esteem. Negative thinking can be compared

31

to having an intruder in your mind that constantly messes up everything, making you feel inadequate, not good enough, and overall bad about yourself and your life. Negative thoughts are often all that it takes to ruin one's self-esteem, which is why it is important to identify toxic thoughts and cut them at the root. Replace the negative thoughts with positive thinking, and you are on the way to increasing your self-esteem. Life is too precious to make yourself your own worst enemy.

Step 5: Avoid Comparisons

Comparing ourselves to how other people look or what others have or can do is a one-way ticket to creating a set of unrealistic expectations that can harm your self-esteem and ruin your chance to become a true Sigma. A Sigma doesn't compare himself to other people – he may have role models and icons, but a Sigma will never compare his life to the life of someone else. Sigmas like to enjoy life and work on tailoring life to suit their needs and wants, which is how they can easily focus on achieving their goals. Sigmas don't care if they are not the best at something if they find joy in that activity and avoid comparing themselves with others who may be better at the same activity. Set your expectations and follow them towards achieving your goals. Your self-respect and self-esteem will grow as you stay true to yourself and your vision of life.

Step 6: Give Yourself a Praise

You may be your own worst enemy when it comes to criticism. If you overly criticize yourself, you are struggling with self-esteem but also with patience. It takes time to embrace positivity and welcome positive changes into your life, so cut yourself some slack, enjoy and live in the moment like a true Sigma, and give yourself praise. Instead of criticizing yourself whenever you make a mistake or fail, start praising yourself for every achievement, however small it may be. Praising yourself will also make you feel better about yourself and motivate you to keep on trying and working hard to implement new and positive changes into your everyday life.

Recreate Yourself

To truly recreate yourself, you need to practice acceptance, self-love, and self-esteem. We recommend working on smaller goals towards achieving greatness day to day until you reach the final stage of your journey towards becoming a Sigma male.

You can reinvent yourself without compromising the things you like and appreciate yourself, while you can also work on improving your positives. Follow these simple steps to complete and finalize the first stage of recreating yourself as a Sigma male who believes in himself and is aware of his capacities and possibilities.

Step 1: Get Rid of the Physical Clutter

Things that we keep and don't use or need just take up the space that we could otherwise use more wisely. They also contribute to the feeling of entrapment and may prevent us from moving on to a more quality stage of our life.

Decluttering is a must on your journey to reinvent yourself as you will make more room for new things to come. It will also be easier for you to find your new self once you get rid of the excess and unnecessary things you have been piling up around your home. You can throw away, donate, recycle, or sell the things that you no longer need or identify with, so start decluttering for a better version of yourself. You are guaranteed to feel instantly better and almost reborn once you clear out all the things that you no longer need.

Step 2: Get Rid of the Emotional Clutter

Emotions can also be piled up as things, having an even worse effect on your mental health and state of mind. Emotional clutter can be defined as a mess of emotions that remain unresolved or misunderstood (by yourself) for a long period. Emotional clutter is more difficult to deal with than physical clutter, of course, as you can't see or physically remove emotions. More often, you don't even understand what is going on in your mind once the emotional clutter starts negatively affecting you.

The best way to deal with emotional clutter is to trace and identify your own emotions whenever you feel like you need to. Start by asking yourself:

"How do I feel right now?" or "How do I feel today?" Try to identify the entire spectrum of emotions you are experiencing at a given moment, then ask yourself: "Is there a reason for this feeling?" or "Why do I feel this way?" The answers to these questions should help you keep track of emotional clutter and negative emotions that should be resolved.

When it comes to a resolution, there is another question to ask yourself: "Can I do something at this moment to make myself feel better?" If there is, you should try and declutter the negative emotions standing in your way. There is always something you can do to declutter. One of the most effective methods is to rationalize negative emotions, make peace with the way you feel, and "replace" the negative emotion with a positive one. When you are feeling blue, try doing something that you particularly enjoy. Planning your future self and listing your goals may also help you feel better.

Step 3: Focus on Positive Things

Regardless of how grim and unwelcoming your day may be or seem to be, there is always a good thing to focus on and look forward to. It is as simple as believing that the next day will be better than the last, and if that isn't the case, then you can always count on the day after tomorrow and the day after that, and so on. The sun will always rise, and each sunrise is a new opportunity for you to shine and start over. Think about your plans rather than reproaching yourself over past failures and mistakes. Focusing on positive things will help you induce the needed positivity into your life in the long run.

This is more difficult than it sounds, but you shouldn't be intimidated by obstacles. Your self-esteem may only rise with your ability to master these obstacles. Go an extra mile for yourself and for the sake of changing your life into a perpetual set of positive thoughts and positive actions.

Step 4: Create a Healthy Routine

Having a routine is important when you are working on becoming the best version of yourself, especially when you are trying to stay away from toxic people and negative thoughts. Create and plan a routine that is healthy for you and you feel comfortable with. Exercising, a healthy diet plan, keeping your place clean, and both productive and fun activities should be a part of your daily routine. Make sure to include your practices and lessons for appreciation, self-love, and self-esteem with other exercises we will provide you with.

The best way to create a valuable and healthy routine that will affect your life positively is to make a list of activities to implement into your daily routine. It is also important to stick to your routine, which requires motivation and dedication. Your greatest motivation may be becoming a true Sigma male.

MINDSET MAKEOVER

We all change. Change is an inevitable thing that you can always count on. Change is also one of the rare certainties we have in life – whether you control the change or the tide of change controls you, life itself is in perpetual motion through the concept of metamorphosis and transformation.

You have a choice to control the way your life is changing to some extent, while you need to accept some changes as somewhat independent and considered out of your control. These changes are more likely to be related to other people and other external factors, while you can, in great part, participate in changes that are connected to your inner self – personality improvements, lifestyle changes, and, of course, changing your mindset.

Changing your mindset is essential for embracing the new you and becoming a true Sigma male who knows what he wants and how to get it. We are sharing several exercises and practices that can help you with your mindset makeover.

Exercise 1: Practice Meditation

Practicing meditation can start from simple breathing exercises to help you settle down your thoughts and explore your mind. Meditation is also beneficial in reducing stress, inducing relaxation, and will also help you transition to a more mindful state.

Start with simple breathing exercises; breathe in and breathe out in equal intervals so that it feels natural to you. We will show you how to meditate, step by step, in one of the following chapters while you are practicing your breathing technique. We recommend finding a peaceful place in your home where you can't be disturbed. Turn off your phone and mute all potential distractions. Whether you put on some relaxing music is up to your preferences – the only thing that matters is to relax and exercise your breathing techniques. A simple breathing technique where you breathe in and out in natural intervals can help you focus and concentrate, as well as relax and relieve the stress you might be dealing with.

Practice for at least 5 minutes a day on two separate intervals for a week, then increase the exercise time to 10 minutes per two intervals. The perfect time of the day for this exercise is anytime, so choose the part of the day that best suits you.

Exercise 2: Work on Self-development

As we discussed earlier in the book, every new day is a new opportunity to explore your possibilities and options and make a step towards improving yourself. Make sure you always have time to work on self-development, so whether you're working on breathing exercises, learning a new language or a skill, you should always have time for yourself. By committing to your goals every day, little by little, you are getting closer to the goal of becoming a Sigma. Sigmas are pretty much aware of themselves and their surroundings, so they know how to utilize this skill to their advantage in terms of self-improvement and progress. Most importantly, make self-improvement your number one priority. Every change begins with a small step, and thousands of small steps make a journey.

Exercise 3: Induce an Epiphany

The definition of epiphany is a moment of great realization and sudden revelation, which is crucial for making lifelong changes that will affect your personality and your daily life. In this case, you want to learn how to become a Sigma who is not afraid to speak his mind and is overall self-sufficient, strong, and focused on self-improvement. Ask yourself a question, "What made me want to change?" Reflect on everything that you have achieved in your life and the things you want to achieve and succeed in. This way, you are inducing an epiphany, which should help you see your possibilities and have an overview of your past experiences and choices.

Now that you've asked yourself a question and provided an answer, what did you learn about yourself? What needs to be changed? What is it that you were doing wrong? How can you make improvements? What needs to be improved?

Let's see what else you can do to trigger a full mindset makeover and learn how to become a Sigma.

List Your Goals

We've already discussed listing goals in earlier sections, where we suggested making a plan to have a clear outlook on what you want to achieve in life. We also recommended working on achieving smaller goals daily towards completing the main goals you have listed – that way; you will gain daily satisfaction, which should motivate you to keep on going until you achieve your dreams. You already have a list of life goals you want to achieve, while you should have another list of goals closely related to your transformation. We have already listed all staple qualities and characteristics of a Sigma male that you should practice and adopt to become one, while you also know which traits are not welcome if you want to go through a full Sigma personality makeover.

Write down all the new traits you would like to have that match the personality of a Sigma male you want to become, so you can work out a plan for getting where you want to be. As with the previous list of life goals, create small goals that you can complete every day for the sake of both satisfaction and progress.

For example, your list should look something like this:

1. *I want to be brave*

Practice:

- *Speak your mind*
- *Express yourself*
- *Make the first move*
- *Take initiative daily*

1. *I want to be decisive*

Practice:

- *Make your own choices*
- *Rely on your wants and needs*

1. *I want to be self-sufficient*

Practice:

- *Spend quality alone time*
- *Work on your goals and improvements (check, already doing it!)*

1. *I want to be mindful*

Practice:

- *Meditate*
- *Reflect on your emotions and motivations*
- *Trace negative thoughts*
- *Embrace positivity*

1. *I want to be attractive*

Practice:

- *Work out*
- *Eat healthily*
- *Keep up with grooming and hygiene*
- *Dress up to feel good*

Add as many makeover goals as needed while also adding practices and activities that can help you achieve your goals, little by little every day. The most important thing to note is that you shouldn't put pressure on yourself – it is important to be consistent, but it is more crucial to follow up with changes and practice under terms that make you feel comfortable. Pressuring yourself may also stress you out and even make you give up on your goals.

Allow Yourself to Grow

When we are kids, we are constantly going through different changes. We grow mentally and physically in a continuous fashion, and we don't even notice. Once we grow up, we change at a slow pace when it comes to physical aspects and growing older; however, we can control the way we change mentally if there is appropriate motivation and dedication. As children, we could accept these changes lighthearted, wanting to be stronger, smarter, and older, while in adulthood, we often associate growth with growing older, which is not a favorite part of adulthood for many.

Growth is often associated with growing older, an irreversible change feared by many adults – we all appreciate youth and all its perks but often forget the perks of growing wiser as we grow older. This is how growth may also be associated with fear, so some people restrain from changing anything about themselves, fearing these changes. Growth is part of a human journey, and we grow from the day we are born to the day we are no longer here. As mentioned before, change is inevitable but is not always bad and doesn't need to be perceived as negative. Some changes – like getting older – can't be controlled, but you can control how you change your mindset and your outlook on the world and yourself. The very fact that you have come this far in the guide means that you are ready to embrace change and everything that comes with it, which is already the first step towards changing – acceptance.

Once you accept yourself and decide to change things you believe should be changed, you will welcome transformation into your life. Allow yourself to grow by expelling the fear of change out of your mind and out of your life.

The Ultimate DOs for Sigma Males

To help you on your journey towards changing your mindset following Sigma male traits and virtues, we are listing the ultimate DOs for the sake of guidance. Let's see the definite DOs in a life of a mysterious Sigma who appreciates independence, values differences, and enjoys working on self-improvement.

1. Spend Quality Alone Time

We have already emphasized the importance of solitude in the life of a Sigma male. To change your mindset to fit the lifestyle and ways of a Sigma, you should try and spend quality time alone. That doesn't mean that you should isolate yourself against your will but rather means that you should try and enjoy your own company whenever you are alone. Spend some quality time with yourself regardless of whether you are just chilling and enjoying idleness or working on improvements. Spending some alone time will allow you to know yourself better, which is more than helpful on your journey of changing your mindset and becoming a Sigma.

1. Speak Your Mind (With Fewer Words)

A part of Sigma's tasteful mysteriousness is due to the appreciation of speaking your mind with fewer words. Sigmas are essentially men of few words; they will try to convey a clear message and express their opinion without convincing others or trying too hard to make other people interested. This aspect allows Sigmas to relieve the pressure that many people have when it comes to communication with other people. Instead of debating and explaining yourself, speak your mind and share your thoughts in a casual way that doesn't pressure you into convincing someone to accept your opinion – what is important is that you respect that others may not agree with everything you say.

A Sigma can tell a lot with only a few words without the need to make someone accept his thoughts and beliefs, which is where his strength lies. So, don't feel that you must explain yourself unless you want to spend more time talking with someone you may like.

1. **Learn More**

Just like you can grow as a person your entire life if you don't choose stagnation, you can always learn something new. Learn more about things that interest you and explore new interests to keep an open mind and introduce diversity to your life. Sigmas love succeeding and achieving goals and are always ready to learn more and gain new experiences. That means that Sigmas also require more personal space to fulfill themselves and pursue their dreams, often placing this need above everything else. Sometimes, "everything else" also includes relationships. A Sigma won't settle with a relationship with a person who doesn't understand this need to always learn, grow, and create new experiences. Learning is important for a Sigma to bloom.

1. **Create Your Own Rules**

You don't need to comply, and as a Sigma, you don't want to or think you have to. In the hierarchy, Alpha is the type that creates standards and sets the rules for others to follow, always competing for attention and depending on validation. Sigmas create their own rules to follow – they don't impose it on anyone, nor express it, but follow their own rules that often defy conventional expectations that other people have for you.

So, for example, if you want to move to another country or start a business of your own and leave your nine to five job and someone tells you, "You can't do that" – they say it because it's some kind of a rule that may be in line with the general conviction of their surroundings, which could be "You can't take such risks." In reality, you can take a risk and have a leap of faith, changing whatever you want in your life, whether that's the country you live in, your job, your surroundings, etc. – anything. That is how you set your standards and your own rules. If you make a drastic change in your life that you believe can change your life for the better, you should consider it regardless of what other people say.

1. **Be Present**

A true Sigma can fully experience every situation and emotion because he can live in the moment. The ability to be present is extremely important for Sigmas, as being mindful allows them to learn more and satisfy their curiosity. Being present and living in the moment is also beneficial as it can reduce the stress after a bad day, while it can also mitigate anxieties over future and everyday problems.

The Ultimate DON'T's for Sigma Males

1. **DON'T Adapt to Other People's Expectations**

This ultimate DON'T is closely related to creating your own rules and setting your standards. You don't need to comply if you don't want to. Other people who may not be considerate with differences will always have expectations carved by their own life experiences.

A problem that some people have is the inability to empathize with people and accept other people's differences, which is not the case with a Sigma. Sigmas acknowledge and appreciate different opinions as they can understand the differences between people and perceptions. This allows Sigmas to understand morale as an ambiguous creation. So, while others may not understand the expectations that you have for yourself, you should focus on your goal and not adapt to their expectations.

1. **DON'T Sabotage Yourself**

You can be your worst enemy if you choose self-reproach over praising yourself and providing the self-validation that your confidence needs. Practice tracing and getting rid of negative thoughts related to fears and not reality. This way, you see a clear version of reality and cut yourself some slack. Don't criticize yourself for every little thing that goes wrong – this way, you are sabotaging yourself, which can negatively affect your progress and self-improvement.

1. **DON'T Indulge in Self-appreciation**

Appreciating yourself is a major perk as it allows you to strengthen your confidence and enjoy life to its fullest. Self-appreciation can also boost your ego, especially when you are doing well without anyone's help, validation, or gratification except for your own. In case you are overly content with yourself, you may display a dose of arrogance that will prevent you from seeing the real self. In this case, it may happen that you completely disregard your negative traits and exaggerate the brilliance of positive ones.

1. **DON'T Fear the Change**

Sigmas don't fear the change – they embrace it and take the best out of it. Change is one of the rare certainties in life as everything changes, including ourselves. Sigmas often find changes exciting and welcome transformation with eagerness.

1. **DON'T Be Pressured into Blending In**

Many people are pressured into fitting in and blending in, while the two concepts are not the same. Fitting in is not a strange thing for a Sigma male – a Sigma can fit in in almost any social group, as Sigmas have broad interests and are usually attractive physically and mentally to other people. Blending in is different, as a true Sigma would never try to blend in and be like everyone else just to fit in. Fitting in is an important social skill, as you can easily make friends and communicate with people, but blending in is, in a way giving up on your individuality for the sake of acceptance.

MENTAL STRENGTH AS AN ATTRACTIVE TRAIT

People who are mentally and emotionally strong are incredibly attractive to others. Many women would rather choose to date a mentally and emotionally strong person over a physically strong individual. Physical strength is, of course, attractive as well, but it is a superficial quality that doesn't offer any value in relationships and intellectual tasks. Aligning the strength of your body with the strength of your mind is a perfect combination. Ancient Greeks believed that physical health is equally important as mental health and that the two combined should be a standard of a healthy and intelligent person – a healthy mind in a healthy body.

Sigmas detest frivolity and superficial qualities, which is why most Sigmas like to focus on building their mental strength; however, it is important not to neglect your exterior, which is your body. "I don't care" Sigmas do care about their bodies after all.

When it comes to mental strength, it is important to thicken your skin regarding how you experience negative and stressful situations and how you resolve and live through problems and complications. A strong body won't help you there, but a strong mind will. Struggling to accomplish something and focusing on your goal regardless of difficulties is a sign of mental strength. We all have problems, and what counts is how we act and react to these problems. Will you resolve the things that trouble you, or will you sink in despair and wait for the worst to pass? The difference in the choice between the two is also the difference between mental strength and weakness.

We share some of the most effective methods and practices to help you build and rebuild your mental strength, which will help you resolve and accept your problems more easily as you complete your transition to Sigma.

Building Mental Strength

Changing and constantly striving to achieve your goals can be stressful and also a major test of your mental strength. Admitting that some things about you need to be improved and changed is also a sign of mental strength. Mental strength is the measure of how well we can handle any situation, particularly stressful experiences.

Like physical strength and fitness, mental fitness can also be practiced, as mental strength is not a trait but rather a process of practicing the strength of your mind and stability of your emotions. Building mental strength thus requires time and practice but should bring many perks to your everyday life once it's achieved, starting from easily handling even the most stressful situations and achieving your goals.

Mental strength reflects our ability to handle negative and stressful situations in life and also shows our resilience in terms of psychological capacity. Mental strength is beneficial when it comes to living your life to the fullest and being able to experience negative situations without letting go of the good things that make you happy and that you have in your life. Mental strength will also help you become a more creative person and help you recognize the opportunities presented to you.

Here are some of the ultimate strategies that can help you build your mental strength and acquire a psychological capacity of a true Sigma male.

#1 Avoid Multitasking

In the modern age, multitasking has become almost a standard regardless of what you do – doing more than one thing at a time may be seemingly productive, but the word "seemingly" is there for a reason, as focusing on multiple things all at once is not productive and won't provide you with best results. Essentially, multitasking is a myth, as our brain just doesn't have the potential to fully commit to more than a single task at a time. You can't utilize all your capacity if you don't focus on one thing. Focus on one thing at a time and live in the present, as this is one of the best strategies for building your mental strength – other tasks and problems can't affect you while you are focused on a single problem that you need to solve.

#2 A Healthy Mind in a Healthy Body

We have already emphasized the importance of having a healthy mind in a healthy body and aligning the progress of both to get the best results. To assure a healthy mind, you also need to take good care of your body, which means exercising and keeping up with an active lifestyle. You don't need to exercise more than 15 to 30 minutes a day, and you can use any routine you like – running, swimming, training in a gym, or just walking – it all works great for building your physical and mental strength. Exercising also encourages the production of serotonin, also known as the hormone of happiness.

#3 Self-care Time as a Must

Self-care time is a definitive must – it will allow you to decompress and enjoy the little things instead of constantly working on completing tasks and achieving goals. Everyone needs a break, and taking a break to enjoy a book, your favorite show, or working on a hobby of yours all count as self-care time. Set aside some time, at least an hour a day, only for yourself.

#4 Visualize the Positive

Visualization is a powerful tool, as it can help you identify the future vision you have for yourself. Envisioning the future outcome of your actions, choices, and decisions is a normal part of, well, being human. We all can't help but consider the outcome of our choices, which is what decision-making is based on. With Sigmas, visualization may be an important part of the deductive process, as it empowers critical thinking. Visualize the positive outcomes over negative ones that can be produced by fears and anxieties about the future. Negative thoughts can result in negative visualization, which may further discourage you from making your own choices like a true Sigma.

#5 Create a Favorable Setup

The first step towards succeeding is preparing yourself for success, or rather setting yourself up for success. But what does that mean, and how do you do it? It's easier and far less complex than you might think, as it all starts with small things. For example, if you plan to become fit and stay fit, you should get rid of all the triggers that may put you off track on your path to fitness. If you want to learn more about something or learn a new skill, sign up for a course or start reading. You can make a list of all activities that you would like to do in a day to make an organized schedule or a general outlook on what you want to achieve. This way, you can be reminded that you are set up for success.

How to Practice and Empower Mental Strength

Practice makes everything better, so we present you with some useful lessons and exercises that will help you practice and empower your mental strength. Start from the five strategies listed in the previous section to set yourself up to increase your mental strength, one of the greatest strengths that describe a Sigma male.

Practice #1: Controlling Emotions

Controlling your emotions doesn't mean that you should mute your feelings and neglect your emotions – it means that you can identify negative emotions and utilize them constructively and positively. Let's say that you feel angry at the moment. What does this anger do for you? Does it make you feel better or solve the problem that made you angry in the first place? No. What anger does is block your attention and divert your focus, so you can't concentrate on the things that matter. What you can do is to divert that anger and turn it into motivation. Being aware of this anger can serve as a reminder of what is important in your life.

Now, you can do this for every emotion, which includes desperation, sadness, fear, frustration, and other emotions that we experience as negative, and that makes us feel uncomfortable. Let's say that something made you sad, and you are feeling blue with no obvious reason to be happy or feel joy. Sadness will demotivate you and prevent you from continuing to try and give your best. You can either wallow in sorrow – which we do not recommend in any circumstance, or you can consider changing things that make you sad, whether that is a person, your surroundings, or your behavior patterns.

Practice #2: A Bit Better Than Yesterday

Every day is a new opportunity that brings a brand-new set of possibilities that you can ignore or reach out for. Treat each day as a new opportunity and a way to become a bit better than yesterday. Micro progress is still progress and will take you a long way in the long run and help you practice your mental strength. You can start with trivial things like reorganizing your wardrobe, cleaning your place, and getting rid of the things you no longer need, or you can start a new course, try a new hobby, or whatever you think would help you do something good for yourself and your future day to day.

Practice #3: Consider New Things

We've just mentioned getting a new hobby or starting a new course, which is another great practice for exercising your mental strength. Leave your comfort zone and try something you've never tried before or do something that you've always wanted to do and never had the time or courage to go through with it. What is stopping you from trying new things and exploring new possibilities? Only you can set your limits, and it is in your best interest not to set boundaries when it comes to learning new skills and trying something new that could improve your life. Trying new things will make you mentally stronger, as you will be prepared for the unexpected and comfortable with the changes that come as a surprise.

#4 Create a Safe Place

Safety is a staple necessity to humans as we all appreciate comfort and enjoy the general feeling of being guarded and protected. Some people find protection from potential harm by keeping their emotions neglected. Some prefer healthier ways of coping with potentially getting hurt – they create a safe place where they can take a break and assess their emotions by identifying the factors causing these negative feelings.

Creating a safe place where you can just vent out all the negativities can help you become mentally stronger, as you can approach your emotional state from the viewpoint of a critical thinker that a Sigma male represents. That way, you can go through potential case scenarios and pick an action that works in your favor – consequently, you are creating a positive reaction, i.e., outcomes. As a huge plus, you will be able to deflect any negativity coming your way in the future.

For example, if you're having a hard time, go on a weekend getaway somewhere where you can appreciate the beauty of nature and all its sounds and sights. Nature can also help us reconnect with ourselves, strengths and weaknesses alike.

#5: Work Towards a Purpose and With a Purpose

Finding a purpose will keep you "anchored" and help you find the motivation needed to achieve your goals and make a change. Whenever you feel like you can't go on and miss completing your daily goals that lead to achieving a major goal, remind yourself of the purpose of getting back on track. Having a purpose means that you are not lost and that you are striving towards something in life. Why do you want to make a change and become a Sigma? Why do you want to learn something new, find a new job, or change your behavior? Once you answer all your "Whys," you will know your purpose.

Finding Your Inner Peace

Stress, anxiety, worry, fears, frustrations, fast-paced days, weekends that seem to be shorter from week to week, and the overall chaos of the modern world call for a state of inner peace. The hectic tempo that many of us have and the difficulties involved in resolving problems can take a toll on anyone after a while, which is why it is important to learn how to find your inner peace.

Inner peace can be described as the state of happiness and content where you are not affected by external factors of chaos and stress. This state is achieved by reconnecting with yourself and peeking into your very essence - your mind and your emotions. Inner peace can be achieved by practicing acceptance, so we recommend revisiting the chapter on Practicing Acceptance to reaffirm the lesson and reinforce that you accept yourself the way you are and the way you want to be.

Now, we have already resolved the problem of what to do to find inner peace, which is to accept yourself, practice self-love, self-appreciation, and exercise your mental strength – but what about the things you SHOULD NEVER do if you wish to find inner peace. Let's see what you should avoid as you are practicing self-acceptance and mental strength to find your inner peace.

1. Happiness is NOT Defined by Achievements

We defined inner peace as the state of happiness, while many of us often associate happiness with things we have and the goals we have achieved. Achieving goals can grant you happiness, but striving for achievement is a never-ending journey – as soon as you have completed one goal, you will find the next one to strive for, and it is almost certain that this will happen again and again and again. Each new goal achieved will lead to creating more goals. But what about the time spent in between achieving your goals – are you only happy when you achieve something?

Happiness can be found within you, which is how inner peace is achieved. Don't fool yourself into believing that you can only be happy once you achieve everything you want, as this philosophy will grant you pressure and some rather unhappy times of struggle. Instead, reflect on what you already have and be thankful for everything you have achieved by far as you are focusing on new achievements.

1. Don't Fear Your Authenticity

Many people try to hide that they are different, some because they fear being judged, and some don't feel comfortable expressing themselves. This is quite the opposite of Sigma philosophy, as Sigmas are not afraid to be authentic and don't mind the judgment, while they are the ones that don't judge in the first place. Once you learn to embrace your authenticity, you will be in a happier place and at peace with yourself. Don't be afraid to show your true emotions and express yourself. Once you reject the fear of being rejected or judged, you will become a more content person.

1. Dominate Your Anger

Anger is one of the most intense feelings considered to be a negative emotion, as it has destructive effects on the person experiencing this emotion. Your anger can't cause anyone to suffer but yourself, eating out the positivity in your life and meddling with your focus. To diminish the effects of anger, you shouldn't act on it or try to suppress the emotion to feel better – you should dominate your anger and use it productively.

Suppressing your anger will take you nowhere and only make you feel worse about yourself, others, and your life in general. Instead, you should own your anger and use it as a creative force. Consider the reasons for feeling angry and turn these into a new plan while anger will be your motivation. It is like taming a wild animal – you should approach it with patience, care, and prudence.

1. **Avoid Comparisons**

We all want to be happy - it is as simple as that. But things are far from simple once we create a "happiness bar" and start comparing the level of happiness we feel with the fabricated idea of how happy we should be. That is how many people compare their state of happiness with other people's happiness as well. This negative behavior can put you down and make you feel bad, even when you are happy, as you might think that you should be happier or that your happiness will soon end.

To find inner peace, you should try and be present when experiencing not only happiness but also other emotions, the good and the bad alike. Practice mindfulness, acceptance, and deal with your emotions with a critical mind and diligence. Enjoy the happy times without comparisons, and you will be a step closer to finding inner peace.

1. **You Don't Need to Be Doing Something All the Time**

Modern people are obsessed with productivity to the extent where many of us feel guilty in idleness. It is perfectly fine to take a break and have a streak of days of just doing nothing about your goals.

How do you feel when you take a break and take a trip to the seaside, for example? You are sunbathing, swimming, maybe meeting some new people, enjoying some free time, etc. You probably take seven to ten days or more on your vacation, feeling refreshed afterward. The same thing goes with selective idleness. You can choose to take a break without feeling guilty about not working on your goals at that moment. Take a break and be present. Live in the moment and place everything on a pause when you feel like you need to get some rest. You will "return" a stronger man in touch with your inner self, which is how you find inner peace.

Meditation can also help you find your inner peace, relax, relieve the stress induced by a hectic life, and prepare yourself for major changes. Let's see how meditation can help you on your journey to becoming a Sigma male.

Meditation and All Its Perks

Meditation has numerous perks, including helping you find the balance you need, finding inner peace, teaching you how to be present, and relieving stress and anxiety. Meditating is also rather simple and easy, as it starts from practicing breathing techniques and letting your mind wander. Meditation will help you relax and pause the things happening around you. There are numerous types of meditations; we will be focusing on Mindfulness meditation and Guided meditation.

Mindfulness Meditation

Mindfulness meditation can help you experience the present and live in the moment by focusing on sensations, emotions, and breathing during the meditative state. The entire goal of this meditation is to help your awareness of self and your surroundings, as well as practice acceptance of your current state of mind and emotions.

Start by finding a comfortable spot in your home where you feel the most relaxed. You will probably need complete silence at the beginning of your meditation practices as you are getting used to meditating, so make sure to choose a time when it's normally peaceful, and there are not many distractions. Start with breathing as already practiced, breathing in and out at a pace that feels natural. You will feel your heart rate slowing down to accommodate the pace of breathing.

As you breathe in and out, focus on the air as it enters and leaves your body. You will feel all sorts of emotions reading your current emotional state, and some of these emotions will probably be negative. Acknowledge these emotions and accept that you are feeling the way you do without actually experiencing the feelings. Imagine that you are a bystander opposed to your emotions, logically inspecting your emotional state. Now, when you've identified your emotions and acknowledged them, you need to let them pass without judging yourself and judging the feelings you are experiencing.

Don't get frustrated if you can't succeed in letting your emotions pass by during the first couple of meditation sessions – this is harder than it sounds, and you shouldn't feel bad about yourself. The important thing is to try and to decide whether Mindfulness meditation is the right thing for you.

Guided Meditation

Guided meditation relies on imagination and visualization. You can use this type of meditation to relax and relieve stress, as well as visualize your goals and the things you want in life. You can use Guided meditation whenever you feel like you need to find your inner peace and just relax - you can describe it as somewhat of a spa day for your mind and soul. The reason why this meditation is called "guided" is because someone, or yourself, should be guiding you on your way to visualizing relaxing experiences and situations.

You can also find guidance in the sounds of nature that you can find online. There are also many audio recordings that people usually find calming – the sound of waves, the wind, rain, birds, and similar sounds that can help you find the calmness you need. You can visualize textures, scents, and scenery as well as sounds, so you can convince your mind that you are where you want and need to be – imagine yourself in the middle of a forest on a warm, sunny day, with birds chirping and a mild wind blowing at your face. You can hear the ocean nearby as the waves are touching the shore. You can imagine any place or situation that makes you feel calm and relaxed.

You can use the same technique to visualize positive outcomes.

What if Meditation Doesn't Work?

Some people find it difficult to enter the meditative state, and the reasons are different - you may be unable to collect your thoughts at the moment or focus on your breathing, or you are just not into meditating, and that is all perfectly fine. That is how some people find various substitutes for meditation to get the same or similar effects. If meditation is not your cup of tea, try hiking or taking long walks surrounded by nature. Another option is music. Listening to music that you like and enjoy can have therapeutic effects on your mind, as music can make us feel a multitude of emotions. Play a song that makes you happy and calm when you are down or move to the sound of your favorite song. You can also pick random compositions that use calming sounds in combination with instruments to relax and collect your thoughts. Music also affects our brain to focus and concentrate, so you can find an ally in the harmony of sounds.

Once you are sure that you've mastered acceptance, mental strength, calmness, self-acceptance, and self-love, and when you have gone through all the lessons in Chapter 1 and Chapter 2, you can dive into the details of the Sigma male law of attraction.

3

CHAPTER 3: THE SIGMA MALE LAW OF ATTRACTION

THE SECRET BEHIND THE SIGMA MALE ATTRACTIVENESS

The most common delusion regarding the life of a Sigma male, specifically the sexual life of a Sigma, is a myth that Sigmas get approached by girls all the time and that they don't have to do anything to win a girl's attention. Yes, that can happen, but even to Betas, Alphas, and other masculine stereotypes like Omega and Gamma boys that have joined the socio-sexual hierarchy. Sigmas indeed have a silent appeal that makes a girl want to approach; however, many girls won't make the first move but will let you know they like you.

The secret behind the attractiveness of a Sigma male lies in his values, which are earned through learning and growing as a person who is ready to improve and experience life to its fullest. That still doesn't mean that a Sigma just has to look at a girl, and she would be all his. No. Girls are not after shiny objects - not all of them, and not many of them – what is valued is the value itself. Sigmas are always ready for new experiences and love to learn, which, by itself, is a good start for offering some kind of value. Let's see some main characteristics of a Sigma male attraction and how these characteristics are sometimes subject to misconceptions.

The Lone Wolf Trope

There is something odd in seeing a person alone in a place where everyone seems to be talking to someone – it is a side-effect of our nature, as we are social "pack animals." Humans would regroup in the distant past to ensure security, food, shelter, safety in numbers, and also to mate, creating thousands-of-years-long social evolution from tribes to civilized societies where we further categorize people into groups by family, coworkers, social circles, etc. Socializing is also crucial for survival in the modern world, which is why solitude is somewhat seen as a sign that something is wrong.

If the person seems to be miserable all by himself, it will most likely send a message to other people that something is wrong with the person or that something happened to the person – a less dramatic scenario is that this person is waiting for someone or has been stood up by a date that never showed up.

On the other hand, if the person is spending the night alone in a restaurant, a bar, or at a party and seems to be enjoying his own company, this might spark some interest among some of the people. This would be an example of the lone wolf trope. The lone wolf here is the Sigma male who is having a great time by himself, confident and unshaken by solitude. This is one of the characteristics of a Sigma male that women find attractive, as it may spark the interest of finding out more about you and why you are all alone. Make yourself present. Try going out by yourself when you feel comfortable about it without any major expectations and see where the night takes you. You can also visit a café for a cup of coffee or take a casual stroll. Anything counts if you feel comfortable.

Building a Unique Style

What do you like to wear? What makes you feel comfortable in your skin? What reflects your personality and shows where you want to be and where you are in life? "Dress to impress" doesn't have to be your normative motto, but you should bear in mind that the way we dress presents our style and expresses our personality, while sometimes clothes can bear even a greater statement and showcase our class, education, and wealth. In this case, we refer to the message you send to others in terms of your character. A way to feel good about yourself is to dress the way you like and feel comfortable with, so go for any style that you feel suits your character the best.

Getting Attention Without Much Effort

Getting attention without much effort doesn't mean you can just walk into a room and all heads immediately turn to you unless you are very attractive physically, which may be the case. Getting attention without trying too much means that it doesn't matter if you are noticed or not. But if you want to get noticed by certain people, the very fact that you have a unique style that expresses a part of your personality and that you have no problems with going out all by yourself is a good start to increase your sex appeal and attractiveness in general. Nothing is done effortlessly, but you can succeed in getting the attention without trying too much. If you have noticed that a girl is looking at you and you are interested in her as well, it's not much effort to make a move and start a conversation, right?

Hard-to-Get

Playing hard-to-get comes naturally to Sigmas, as they don't pretend they are hard to get even if they are. Sigmas are less likely to postpone their activities for someone or prioritize someone over their own time. Sigmas set their tempo and pace and are thus hard to get. When you meet someone special who shares some of your philosophies and the way you see life, that person should understand that you prioritize more value on your own time than the time spent with someone else. Perhaps we all have that one soul mate who functions similarly as we do or whose differences can perfectly align with our characteristics?

When talking about sole physical attractiveness, hard-to-get is a perfect game in multiple scenarios, as people often tend to have an increased interest in what is out of their reach.

Experience the Present, Live in the Moment

We have mentioned the importance of being present and living in the moment more than several times and across multiple lessons precisely because it is so important for your journey towards becoming a Sigma male. Living in the moment is more a state than a characteristic, making Sigmas attractive to the opposite sex. By living in the moment, you experience the present without prejudice or plans, which can set you up for success with ladies. The energy of being present radiates as anyone you talk to can tell that you are invested in your conversation, which is important when trying to attract someone you like. Try living in the moment as soon as you set yourself up for a night out and consider that everything and anything is possible, which will make your encounters even more interesting.

Set Your Goals Straight

It is important to decide what you want in a romantic relationship. Are you looking for a partner who shares your lifestyle and has similar philosophies regarding life, or are you looking for fun? Ask yourself, are you ready to share your time and mind with someone in the long run, or do you just want to experience new things with new people? Even though you are self-sufficient as a Sigma, everyone appreciates love and affection, especially from a person that you like. Set your goals straight, and set your mind for what you need and don't settle for less. It is only fair to the other person that you are straight with your intentions, so showing your true colors is important in not misleading the other person. Sigmas are not players to toy with other people, which is why it is important to be honest about yourself.

SIGMA MALE GAME DECODED

Sigmas are introspective rather than introverted, although some of their characteristics may make people believe that they are dealing with introverts. This trait allows a Sigma male to know himself inside out, which is attractive to many women, especially those tired of dealing with superficial guys who are delusional about their strengths and weaknesses.

When it comes to Sigma's male dating game, there isn't a magic trick specifically reserved for Sigmas to win over a girl they like – the key to the dating game in Sigma style lies in the very essence of his characteristics. A Sigma is a mysterious guy who doesn't talk too much but talks with a purpose and will share his thoughts and opinions with a person they like, not to impress her but to learn new things and see things from a different perspective. Sigmas are also brave and not afraid to make the first move if they are interested in a girl. Sigmas don't play hard to get - they ARE hard to get because they place value on their alone time and personal growth. It is personal growth and the desire to learn more and improve that is so attractive to women. What is even more attractive is that Sigmas are not driven by the desire to be liked. What is there not to like about all these traits, right?

So, your "game" won't be based on making strategies on what to say or what to do for a girl to like you but will be focused on improving yourself and getting where you want to be in life. In most cases, there is nothing more attractive than a man who is aware of himself, isn't afraid of improvement, and knows what he wants in life.

Appreciating Yourself

Hopefully, by now, you have learned to appreciate yourself through numerous practices and exercises we have compiled for you in previous sections. You can use this section to revise what you've learned about yourself. Have you learned to appreciate yourself with all your flaws and traits? If so, have you learned to accept yourself for who you are and change the things that you don't want in your life?

It takes courage to appreciate yourself as you are aware of all the things that can be characterized as negative about you. So you have the power to change these things and become a better person for your own sake, not for the sake of how other people see you. The very fact that you are working on improving yourself provides you with a value that is attractive to other people, so focus on yourself and achieving your goals. If you are happy with yourself, it will be easy for you to make someone else happy, too, and be happy with someone else.

Don't Get Easily Bothered

So, you've made a move, and you got rejected. What now? You can use this experience to analyze what might have gone wrong and step up your game the next time you decide to approach someone. The important thing is not to get easily bothered. There are many reasons why you might have been rejected, and many of those reasons probably don't have anything to do with you. Maybe you made a move on a girl already dating someone, or just isn't interested in dating anyone now, or she just doesn't like you. There's no harm in being rejected other than having a hurt ego, and as a Sigma, your ego is not boosted by other people's acceptance and gratification.

Enjoying New Experiences

Talking to a girl you like is also a new experience and can lead anywhere – the experience can either be negative, positive, or even neutral as you might not be affected by the encounter. The "worst" thing that can happen is to get rejected, but that is not nearly as bad as not trying at all.

Attracting Women

How do Sigmas attract women? As we've mentioned before, there is no magic trick that Sigma can use to make the girl he likes to fall for him, which means that you need to try or at least show that you like that girl standing in the corner with a friend. If she is already looking at you, that is a perfect setup, as you can show her that you are interested in looking back at her and showing your interest. If you maintain eye contact with her, she would probably like you to approach her, which won't be a problem if you have embraced the philosophy of a Sigma – be brave, be present, be mindful.

If you can't make any contact with the girl unless you approach without certainty that you are the point of her interest, you will mostly be relying on self-confidence and perhaps a bit of luck. If you are physically attractive according to the general standards of masculine beauty or have a certain charisma characteristic of Sigma types, it may be easier for you to approach as you may play on the card of good looks. Still, it is not all in good looks as you need to interest the girl in talking to you. Sigmas usually detest generic pickup lines, as they value uniqueness and authenticity, so you can use any conversation starter that you think would reflect your personality. Sigmas always want a girl interested in them because of who they are and not who they pretend to be. Authenticity and honesty are some of the key traits that Sigmas use to interest women.

Strong Beliefs and Philosophy of Sigma Life

The fact that a Sigma wouldn't trade his beliefs for the sake of others is an attractive trait by itself. When combined with the philosophy of self-growth, improvement, and perpetual progress, we have a winning combination with ladies. Some universal traits are appreciated among women regardless of their age, beliefs, and various personality traits and factors. Some of these attractive traits are confidence, independence, self-awareness, motivation to learn, the ability to adapt, and the choice not to. All these traits combine to create a stereotypical male classified as Sigma is rather attractive to women and beneficial to Sigma himself.

The philosophy of Sigma life mostly revolves around self-improvement and creating a life of value. Sigma values new experiences, new lessons, and never-ending learning, always hungry for more. Your strong beliefs, self-awareness, mental strength, and "what happens, happens" attitude are some of your greatest attributes in the dating game – you just need to use them wisely. Don't be afraid to show your true self, and if others like you for it, that is all right. If they don't, that is perfectly fine – don't change for the sake of others; change for yourself and your goals.

"I DON'T CARE" SIGMAS DO CARE ABOUT THEIR APPEARANCE

Sigma usually looks neat and has a unique style, not necessarily eccentric, but you can notice that he is wearing that same jacket that Alpha wears, which somehow suits him differently – basically, it's all about the little details and the attitude. Alpha boasts and likes to be seen, and Sigma usually walks into the room without caring to be seen and somehow gets noticed. How?

People who are confident reflect their confidence by simply being sure about who they are and what they want in life. You know how you can sense when someone is nervous even if they try not to show it? The same thing goes with confidence and other traits and emotions. Alpha's confidence can also be sensed, although this confidence reflects on Alpha's image differently than it would on a Sigma male, mostly because Alpha's confidence is driven by his ego and the validation of others. Alpha enters a room as if he owns it, and Sigma enters the same room as if he has already been there, and everything looks familiar. This is how the "I don't care energy" is achieved. Sigmas DON'T care if they get noticed or not. However, they do care about how they look, as to some extent, your appearance reflects your personality and the things you want in life.

Look Good, Feel Better

We've already discussed how looking good can make you feel better as you are setting yourself up to feel better by simply feeling comfortable with the way you look. This case can be compared to method acting. Method actors take over the personality of the character they play as soon as they put on their character's costume. They become that character by identifying with his style and the outfit that suits the character's personality.

Go through your wardrobe and pick the clothes that you think describe you and your style the best. You may even buy some new clothes if your budget allows it and change your style a bit if you feel like doing so. The saying "A suit doesn't make the man" is not completely accurate, as in a way, what we wear reflects our personality and our inclinations. Don't be afraid to embrace authenticity and express yourself through a medium of fashion.

Good Health is Half the Confidence

Looking good also means taking care of your body and health. Good health is half the confidence, as a healthy and clean man who takes care of his hygiene is more than attractive. Exercise, take care of your hygiene, have regular health checkups, and don't neglect your mental health. A healthy mind and a healthy body are blessings that shouldn't be neglected or taken for granted. An unhealthy lifestyle may take away all the progress you've made, so keep your health in check and take care of your body.

Inducing Mysterious Qualities of Sigma Males

Sigmas are perceived as mysterious and even intriguing, but do Sigmas induce this mystery on purpose? The answer is more likely NO. Behind this perception is a common practice of Sigmas not to talk too much and share only what they think is necessary. Sigmas are direct and dislike oversharing – you will never hear a Sigma sharing his entire life story to someone, especially to a stranger, while Sigmas are always direct in conversations. You will hear exactly what a Sigma thinks, which is a refreshing change. Sigmas don't say what they think other people want to hear – they speak concerning their own beliefs, thoughts, and opinions.

The fact that a Sigma is likely to go out to a bar or a restaurant alone does add to the factor of mystery and intrigue alongside the case of refusing to ramble on for no reason – random chatting is not what a Sigma prefers, which somewhat falls out of the frame of the expected, making Sigmas mysterious to other people.

WHY SIGMAS CARE ABOUT THEIR PHYSICAL APPEARANCE

Physical appearance, regardless of your grade of attractiveness under general beauty standards, tells a lot about you when it comes to the first impression. While Sigmas don't care how other people perceive them, they do care how they look in the light of being content with themselves and their appearance.

Looking good for Sigmas means they feel good and want to feel good about themselves and where they are in life, so physical appearance is in no way neglected. Here are some basics you need to know as a Sigma when it comes to the way you look and how other people perceive you.

The First Impression Matters

The first impression is important, even though you may not care about how other people see you and perceive you. Regardless of your indifference towards other people's opinions, you should look your best for your own sake. In addition, when you like a girl, you can't lie to yourself that you don't care what she thinks about you and whether she likes you or not. Claiming otherwise would be lying to yourself. Just like any other goals you have set for yourself and are working to achieve, you should set yourself up for success when going out and meeting people. First impressions do matter, as it may be your only shot with someone.

Express your true self without reservations and without the fear of being judged and rejected. If you care about that girl liking you, you should show your interest and express your personality with no filters as a true Sigma would. If she likes you back, you may have someone to talk to without having to involve yourself in meaningless small talk that's usually a part of meeting someone for the first time. Be present and enjoy the moment that might take you somewhere great.

Sexual Attraction of Sigmas

Most men will approach a girl with meaningless small talk or a generic pickup line, which the girl has most likely heard before and is probably tired of chitchatting for no good reason. Considering differences, some people enjoy small talk and consider it a normative part of a conversation – but not Sigmas. If a Sigma is talking to someone, he is direct and is not sharing the entire process of forming his opinions, conclusions, and decisions – he keeps these processes to himself and only shares the core of what he wants to say, making a clear point that can be very refreshing to other people. Speaking directly is also sexy to many women, while a part of the sexual attraction of Sigmas lies in their confidence to say what they think and speak directly.

So, we have a man who is not afraid of taking the initiative, not afraid of speaking his mind, a man who accepts changes as a natural and healthy part of life, who doesn't seek validation and gratification, who is not afraid to chase his dreams and be himself, and who is willing to learn and experience new things. Sigma is honest in his authenticity and is looking for a person of his likeness who is independent and open to new experiences. In conclusion, the very core of Sigma's personality is sexually attractive, as most women appreciate an independent man who knows what he wants in life and is not afraid to speak his mind. This is truly refreshing in comparison to men who only speak what they think women want to hear and can't deliver on their words and promises. Living your life with honesty and awareness that you are not perfect is very sexy! It's all about the energy you reflect by solely working on improving yourself.

Lone Wolf Vibe and Confidence

The lone wolf trope is a huge part of the attractiveness of a Sigma male, and this phenomenon can be easily broken down and explained through a simple example. Let's say that you see someone alone at the bar – it can be a girl – and she doesn't look like she is waiting for someone or something. She is just there, present in the moment and looking like she is in good company, even though she is alone. It is like seeing a group of popular kids in high school, full of confidence and looking like they are having fun – secretly, you want to be around them because you want to feel like they do, which is perfectly content and happy with yourself and your place in the world. Even though our "example girl" is all alone at the bar, she radiates the same energy that makes you want to approach her and know more about her. The secret in this attraction is not in how you perceive this girl, but in the way she feels about herself, which is confident and happy with who she is.

Now, replace the girl in the scene with a guy – this guy is you as a Sigma, the lone wolf with the confidence of a pack.

KEEPING UP WITH HYGIENE AND HEALTH

It is very important to take good care of your mind and equally important to take care of your body and hygiene. Do you like the sight of someone who doesn't care about how they look or don't care about their hygiene? Of course not, as self-care and good health are equally as attractive as being confident. Just like wearing that outfit you like makes you feel good about yourself, being healthy and clean can help you boost your self-confidence and feel better.

The feeling of entering the shower and letting the water flow is priceless and can also help you in your pursuit of positivity. Aside from the obvious perks of being clean and smelling great, you can use your shower time to reflect on your day and visualize washing off all the negatives. Let the water flow over your body as you imagine all the negative things just being washed away with it. Empower yourself through the little hygiene and beauty rituals that you have. Taking care of your hair, body, health, and how you look will make you feel better and set you up for success.

Working Out

Working out is more than just staying fit. Exercising encourages the production of serotonin and dopamine, as well as epinephrine. Dopamine is a hormone naturally present in our body and affects our brain to feel motivated, fulfilled, and content. Serotonin is the hormone of happiness, and epinephrine is a hormone naturally released in our body when we are under physical or emotional stress to prepare us with increased muscle strength and adrenaline. So, there are more perks of working out than "just" looking fit.

You don't need to engage in rigorous workout plans and direct your focus towards getting fit as if your life depends on it unless you enjoy it and want to make exercising a great part of your everyday routine. If you just want to stay fit and feel good about yourself while working on your fitness and wellbeing, you don't need to spare more than 30 minutes per day to achieve your goal.

Swim, walk, run, jog, do cardio at home or pick a local gym where you can use different equipment to boost your workout routine. Make exercising your daily routine and pick a time of the day when you can work out for at least 30 minutes. You can try exercising in the morning to boost your mood early on, or you can cut to exercising midday or in the evening. It is important to pick a time that's most convenient and most comfortable for you.

Eating Healthy

A healthy diet is a big part of a healthy lifestyle, plus healthy and tasty food will make you feel great about yourself. You can visit a professional nutritionist and see which diet regimen would suit you the most from a medical perspective, or you can start by removing unhealthy products from your kitchen pantries, like greasy and junk food, unhealthy snacks, and sugar-saturated delights that don't have such delightful effects on your body.

Start by motivating yourself into putting this new diet regimen to work by removing all the temptations and balancing the calories and nutrients your body needs. Make sure to accommodate your dietary needs to your workout regimen. Even if you are not struggling with weight or have an eating disorder, you should keep your diet in check.

Dress to Impress – The Silent Heartthrob

Dress to impress yourself in the first place. Once you are satisfied with the way you look, the chances are you will also become a point of positive impression. And even though you generally don't care about being accepted or care about the way others perceive you, if you want to get yourself noticed by a girl you like, you do care about the way you look. Mainly because you want to feel good about yourself, which is perfectly fine. Your clothes can make a great first impression based on your style, sense of fashion, and authenticity in expressing yourself.

DOs and DON'Ts of Attraction

Let's see how some of the main DOs and DON'Ts regarding attraction can help you step up your dating game and seduce that girl you like.

(DO) Listen

Sigmas are great listeners, first because they are direct and don't involve themselves in meaningless chitchatting. Second, they respect other people's opinions and are interested in seeing things from different perspectives. Use this skill when you are talking to a girl, as listening can tell you a lot about the person you are socializing with. Listening can also show you whether your potential partner is all about talking and wanting to be heard or if she also appreciates other people's opinions.

(DON'T) Forget to Be Present

Listening also involves being present, which you have practiced in some of the previous lessons. Experience the moment you are having with the girl you are interested in, and don't think about any expectations that you might have had or still have. Just live in the moment and talk to her if you feel that you can connect on some level. Even if this is only a one-time thing and you will never see each other again, immerse in the talk and experience the present moment.

(DO) Express Yourself

If the girl you are interested in also knows how to listen and asks the right questions, don't be afraid to express yourself. Remember the exercises and practices involving mental strength and self-confidence that should have prepared you for expressing your true self regardless of things that you might not be proud of.

(DON'T) Try to Impress Her

Expressing yourself means being your true self in front of others, regardless of how you feel about someone. You shouldn't feel the need to apologize for anything that makes you who you are if you respect others the same way you want to be respected. No matter how much you like someone, never try to impress them by pretending to be something you are not. If that person is interested in you, she will be impressed by your true self.

(DO) Follow up with Body Language

Flirting with someone and socializing with people, in general, involves communication that goes beyond words – our body and the way we move, walk, and talk, and even observe our surroundings can also tell a lot about us –this is known as the language of the body or body language. In the next chapter, we will introduce you to some of the basic body language lessons, so you can learn how to act on what people say without words. Reading body language can tell you if someone is bored, interested, honest and help you see all the intricacies of human interaction.

(DON'T) Fear Rejection

We have already mentioned fear of rejection as a huge demotivational factor in taking action. Fear can paralyze us and demotivate us, preventing us from acting upon our wants and needs. Ask yourself, what is the worst thing that can happen if you approach a girl and she rejects you? The worst thing is probably being rejected in this entire scenario. So, what if you get rejected?

You can use this experience of rejection to become more resilient and stronger than you were before rejection. One thing is for certain; you will never know if you don't try.

Now that you've learned something more about the law of Sigma male attraction, you can move onto the next chapter where we discuss seduction and being seduced by a Sigma male.

4

CHAPTER 4: BEING SEDUCED BY A SIGMA MALE

W hile other socio-sexual types in the male hierarchy may create elaborate strategies to seduce a girl, Sigma males are usually set on a different path, working on self-improvement, which is simultaneously your greatest strategy of seduction.

Through the entire guide, we've been emphasizing the importance of working on self-improvement, motivation, self-acceptance, self-love, self-confidence, and self-respect to teach you how to be a true Sigma. All the lessons have led to the point where you can learn how to use everything you know to grow as a person and achieve your goals and help you get rid of your fears and doubts.

Once you are at peace with yourself and are working hard to achieve your goals, the "game" of Sigma seduction should come naturally to you. Let's see how a Sigma usually makes a move when he is interested in a girl, how he talks and sparks interest, and what is hidden behind the charm of an irresistible Sigma.

MAKING A MOVE

As we've said before, girls generally like Sigmas without even knowing much about this hierarchical type of male and the very ranking of males by these socio-sexual standards; however, that doesn't mean that Sigmas just walk into a room, and all the girls are swept off their feet. The reality of this case is rather different. Sometimes, perhaps more than just sometimes, you will be approached by a girl, and you can make a call on whether you would like to engage in a conversation or not. But what happens when the other side is the one that makes that decision?

Let's see how a Sigma male usually makes a move when his interest is sparked.

Evaluate the Situation

Sigmas are critical thinkers, as you already know, which means they like to evaluate situations and consider all the factors involved. As a true analyst, a Sigma will try to pick up any sign that the interest they have is mutual. However, Sigmas are also brave and like to take the initiative, so they can choose to make a move even without any sign that may reveal whether the girl they are eyeing is interested in them.

Don't Overthink

Evaluating situations can easily take you to overthink the situations and imagine all possible outcomes of your action, i.e., what will happen if I approach the girl and make a move? You can be rejected, you can be welcomed with a smile, you may end up talking to that girl for hours, or you can even end up having a coffee or lunch tomorrow. But who knows, perhaps you will realize that she is not what you thought she would be before you made a move, so you lose interest. There are many possibilities, and thinking through each one may take you on a spiral of overthinking the situation. Don't overthink – evaluate the situation in brief and make a move.

Assert Your Presence in Sigma Male Style

You want to get noticed, but you are just not comfortable with how Alphas or Betas assert their presence or seek attention. That is perfectly fine, as you are, after all, a Sigma male type. You don't want to boast and enter the room as you own it, and you also don't want to comply and sit in a corner wallowing over solitude and hoping that a girl will approach you.

Asserting presence as a Sigma can hardly be described as aggressive or planned. Sigma is equally confident as an Alpha would be, but in the case of Sigma, there is no boasting or asserting dominance. You need to rely on your energy and mindfulness to make you stand out, for which you should work on improving the image you have of yourself. Be who you are, and your presence will surely be noticed by the right people, while you can always choose to make the first move and rely on your confidence.

A Mindful and Casual Approach

Talking about approaching with confidence, you also need to employ the mindfulness you have learned to evaluate the situation properly and become aware of all the factors that make a certain situation as it is. Being mindful means that you have learned not to be overly reactive to new experiences so you can make logical decisions with a cool head.

When approaching a girl, immerse in the present and don't think about potential outcomes – try going with the flow solely based on your personality and the concept of mindfulness where you are fully aware of your situation and the experience you are going through. This will allow you to focus on what is important as you start a conversation with a girl you are interested in. First, ask yourself why this girl interests you – the answer to this question could be your conversation starter. Be direct in your approach but also approach casually without putting pressure on the situation with great expectations.

Pay attention to how this girl acts and reacts to your approach and the very fact that you are walking towards her – keep eye contact to show her your interest as you casually approach with a direct question.

THE SIGMA MALE TALK

Sigmas love to talk, although they rarely talk if they feel they don't have a good reason to spill words or are not motivated or interested in the conversation. Sigma will rarely use excess words and avoids meaningless chitchatting. At the same time, he usually has a wide range of topics that interest him, making him a great person to talk to - of course, if he is interested in talking. Let's see how a typical Sigma communicates when he likes a girl and how you can use seduce the girl you like.

A Talkative Loner

Although Sigmas are perceived as loners, they like to talk if they believe the story is leading somewhere. Chitchatting and small talk is not Sigma's cup of tea, so they will likely lose interest or won't talk at all – small talk just seems like a huge waste of time. Given that you've been working on yourself by learning new skills and immersing in new knowledge on your way to becoming who you want to be, luckily, you have a lot to talk about. Do you have an interesting hobby, a captivating point of view or conclusion that you feel like sharing? If so, don't be afraid to share your opinion as you are having a conversation with a person you found interesting at first sight.

Share your opinion, listen and talk back – once again, be fully present and enjoy the moment.

Make Her Approach You

We can talk with more than just using words, and later in this chapter, we will show you how to read some expressions in body language. For now, you should know that you can make a girl approach you with some simple body language techniques. Make sure that your body is facing the person of interest or that she can at least see you in the crowd. Glance at the girl a couple of times while trying to show your interest but be careful to do it casually - not overly seductive. Also, you shouldn't stare at her for too long as she might think that you are being creepy, which is what you don't want. Catch a glimpse of her while you are trying to tell her something with her eyes. Think about what you would talk to her about every time you look at her, and if she looks back, she may be able to pick up the signs.

This is how you can make a girl approach but be aware that in the society we live in, it's expected that the guy approaches the girl, so don't be surprised if the girl is looking at you with the same interest you have for her but doesn't approach you in the end.

Keeping Her Interested

If the girl does approach you or you decide to approach her and start a conversation, you should keep her interested for as long as you wish the conversation to turn into something more. The best way to keep a girl interested is to show interest in what she has to say and to validate her opinion – of course, there is no good reason to validate her opinion if you don't get along, or your opinions are far different, but you can always show respect for different stances and beliefs.

Listening is a great part of the deal of keeping her interested, as you will be able to find out more about her and share some similarities or similar points of view that you might have. If you've managed to find a girl you think is perfect to date and talk to, then you should share some of your thoughts with her. Share an interesting story you think she might like, but only concerning what she is talking about and in the natural course of the conversation. If she's anything similar to you, she will know how to listen, too, and ask the right questions.

Another strategy of keeping her interested is to provide only "teaser" thoughts. For example, if she asks you what you do for a living, you can tell her something about your job without revealing everything about your position at work. Don't overshare, while the details you do share should be tastefully picked to reflect the core of the answer to her questions.

Sharing Your Thoughts

Share some of your thoughts but avoid oversharing and going into the details of how you come up with a certain conclusion – rattling and boasting is not part of a Sigma personality. Sigma is likely to choose concise sentences that reveal the point without saying too much and without explaining the story behind every sentence. Almost any thought you share should look like it's been well thought through, which should reveal your unintrusive confidence and self-esteem. This shouldn't be a difficult task for a well-read Sigma male who enjoys spending time learning and thinking.

Sharing your thoughts should also convince her that you are enjoying the conversation and that you would like it to continue, which could end in setting up a date.

Handling Rejection

What if your approach didn't go well, and your thought sharing and talking didn't interest her enough as you hoped it would? We've already discussed potential rejection and that the worst thing that could happen when you are rejected is that you've been silently or openly told NO.

How to handle rejection when it happens? A Sigma likes to observe life as a series of challenges and lessons that can make him stronger for better or for worse. A true Sigma can grow and improve in any situation and environment and is usually practicing resilience to factors and experiences that can hurt him. The same goes for rejection. Where did you go wrong? What went wrong? The answer might be nowhere and nothing. Perhaps you weren't her type, and perhaps you were too excited about talking to her and forgot all about mastering mindfulness and approaching casually. Whatever the reason for being rejected, you can analyze the situation tomorrow with a cold mind and learn something new about dating and yourself.

THE SIGMA MALE CHARM

The Sigma male archetype is known as the rarest in the socio-sexual hierarchy of men and as such, is known by an exceptional dose of charm. This charm is mostly unfiltered and unregulated by a Sigma who doesn't perceive himself as charming - he is just being himself unintentionally and unapologetically, but he is himself with intention. A part of this charm is owned by the fact that a Sigma male is perfectly fine on his own, is independent, knows how to set his priorities straight, and is ready to learn and admit that he is not perfect – although he won't admit it directly, despite being direct in conversation. He might slip it casually, though – Sigma style.

We've said it enough by far but being yourself is a core of your charm as a Sigma as it takes being brave to own your life and your decisions.

Sigma Body Language

Sigmas are reserved when observed through the point of body language – they look closed in as opposed to being open for a conversation, and many people perceive them as unapproachable, which is often a part of their charm when it comes to winning ladies' hearts.

As a Sigma, you don't use many hand and body gestures because almost every thought you say out loud is well-thought-through and analyzed. Sigmas like precision, so they often look neat and will share the thoughts they consider can provide some sort of value to other people. Sigmas don't like to be told what to do and take pride in things they know and in the extent of their knowledge in certain areas of their interest, which is how most Sigmas stand tall and look proud wherever they are. Your posture as a Sigma reflects confidence, as you are certain in things you know and are not afraid to look people in the eye; however, eye contact is often brief and focused.

Sigmas seem calm and look calm and collected because that is what they are – focused and fully aware of themselves and their surroundings, thanks to the mind of a cold-headed analyst. They can often be perceived as aloof or cold, even though they don't have any motivation to be superior in comparison to other people. They don't care for other people's validation, but they also don't think that other people should depend on their validation.

When observing a Sigma male, his face is always set up straight with a fixated point of view. They look straight in the eye of the person they are talking to, reflecting confidence and calmness with their chin up. They don't look around and rarely lose their focus. A Sigma may also direct their eyes up, almost looking at the ceiling when they are deeply lost in their thoughts.

Sigmas have a calm demeanor, which is why it is often difficult for other people to read them. On the other hand, some Sigmas are likely to unintentionally show that they are experiencing negative emotions by biting their lip. When silent, Sigma's lips are usually pressed tight as if he is displeased. His head is slightly tilted up while his body weight is evenly balanced, so he looks like he is ready for action, which he is. Sigmas never hunch their backs and tend to stand up straight as if proud. The only time a Sigma doesn't look as calm as usual is when he is brainstorming – in this case, they could play with a pen or an object or play with their fingers. When a Sigma trusts someone, he may use more gestures with his hands and laugh louder than he normally does.

Reading Body Language

Now that you have had the usual body language of a Sigma deciphered and read, let's see how you can read other people's body language that is commonly expressed and unanimously shared by different types of people.

- Lack of eye contact

The lack of eye contact may indicate more than one thing, including shyness, dishonesty, boredom, deceit, and lack of interest.

- Increasing blinking

Increasing blinking can mean that the person is under stress or that he/she is thinking, deeply caught up in his/her thoughts. If the person is under stress, other signs will be involved, like touching their own hands, a sign that they subconsciously need comfort.

- Focused eye contact

If the person is looking at you directly, they are interested in you or what you have to say, or they find your appearance interesting.

- Smiling

Many types of smiles can be grouped into two basic categories – genuine and fake. A smile is a clear sign that a person is happy to see you, and it would be a genuine smile if all face muscles were used. On the other hand, weak smiles that include only moving the lips are most likely fake.

- The proximity of the body

You can tell if someone is interested in you or talking to you or feel comfortable with your presence if their body is to your body – if a person is sitting or standing close to you, they feel comfortable around you and might be interested in you. If you approach and notice that the person is moving away from you or backing up, that is a clear sign that your company is not welcome or the person is uncertain about your intentions.

- Nodding

If a person is nodding slowly while you are having a conversation, the person is listening to you. If the person is nodding rapidly, that likely means that they don't have much time to spare on a conversation or are impatient or not truly interested in the conversation. Fast nodding can also be a sign of agreeing.

- Mirroring

Mirroring means that a person you are sitting next to or talking to is mimicking your behavior, more specifically, your body language. For example, if you start touching your face during a conversation, the person you are talking to does the same thing as a reflex. Or, if you place your elbow on the table while you are talking, and the person follows up with the same gesture only seconds later. If someone mirrors you, they are not doing it as a planned action but as a reflex. This is a sign that the person wants to find a connection with you.

- Feet

Feet and the direction in which the person is pointing with their feet can also reveal non-verbal messages, even they are good at controlling their facial expressions and gestures. People tend to unintentionally point their feet in the direction they would like to go, whether they are sitting or standing. Take a glance and see where the feet of a person you are talking to are directed. If the feet are pointing at you, the person is more interested in talking to you. If they are pointing their feet elsewhere, they probably can't wait to leave.

- Hands

Hand gestures may also reveal a lot about the person you are talking to. If someone is touching their face or nose or playing with their hands, they are more likely under stress or nervous. If they are pointing with their hands at you while gesturing, they are more likely to care about your opinion or have an affinity for you. If someone is supporting their head with a single hand under their chin or cheek, they are focusing as they listen to you, but if they are holding both hands to support their head, they are probably bored.

- Arms

The way people hold their arms can also reveal a lot about them during a conversation. If their arms are crossed, they can be defensive, vulnerable, anxious, or just don't feel like talking to you. If this position of arms is combined with a genuine smile, that person is strong and confident. If a person is holding their arms on their hips, that probably means they are subconsciously asserting dominance.

Deciphering Sigma Charm

A Sigma male is a social chameleon and one of the rarest types in the established socio-sexual hierarchy of dominance – he can easily adapt to any situation and often chooses not to adapt. As we break down all the traits that make a Sigma male one of the most desirable types among women, check how many of these characteristics you have.

A true Sigma is charming because:

- He doesn't care about other people's expectations – a Sigma values expectations that he has for himself.
- He doesn't comply with the traditional social norms – a Sigma doesn't care about who is Alpha, who is Beta, or what society wants him to be.
- He doesn't need validation – a Sigma doesn't seek validation from other people as he does everything with a purpose and not for being accepted.
- He doesn't boast – a Sigma won't praise himself in front of other people and talk about his achievements unless asked, as he is modest.
- He doesn't open easily – a Sigma won't share his thoughts and secrets with just anyone, as you need to earn his trust and affection to open up to you.
- He could be a leader – a Sigma could be a leader just like an Alpha but chooses to be a lone wolf. If a Sigma assumes a high position, he won't act, as he has the entire world under his feet.
- He changes for himself – a Sigma won't choose to change himself for others, as he values his lifestyle and freedom, but he will change for himself.

81

- He is confident – Sigmas invest a lot of their time in learning and developing new skills and spending time on self-improvement, which is how they form their confidence.
- He appreciates personal space – Sigmas like spending time alone, often lost in their thoughts, brainstorming ideas, and learning more. Personal space is very important for a Sigma.
- He is intelligent – Sigma is fully aware of himself and the world around him and understands how people function. He likes adopting new skills and learning new things.
- He is independent – a Sigma will rarely ask for help. They value their independence and love doing things on their own.
- He is respected and respectable – Sigmas respect other people and the differences between people and is often respected for his directness, honesty and that he values other people
- He is mysterious – a Sigma will never reveal his entire life story to a person and will rarely talk about himself. Even when asked, a Sigma will communicate in concise sentences, revealing as little as possible. When he knows something, he will say it, but he won't provide an explanation, considering it redundant.

All of these traits are part of Sigma's undeniable charm and the reason(s) why many women are attracted to Sigma males. You are an independent man who doesn't seek validation and doesn't care about social norms. You respect others and like to do things on your own without imposing your opinion on others. You can adapt to any situation, including social interactions. You approach problems with calmness and a critical mind, always looking for the best solution and a way to excel.

Be aware of your qualities and use them to improve your life and make the best out of what you are given.

5

CHAPTER 5: MAINTAINING INTEREST

I f any of the strategies for meeting and approaching the girl you like
succeeded, the next stage is maintaining interest if you wish to take your
connection to another level. If you like someone, you will most certainly
try to keep them close to you and try to balance your need to be alone, do
your own thing and spend time with your partner. As a Sigma, you like to be
alone with your thoughts and place a lot of value on your daily routines, but
what happens if you like someone that much that you want to share some of
your time with them?

Let's see some strategies that can help you connect with your partner or
potential partner if you have only begun dating without losing your true self
and without compromising your independence.

FLIRTING

Flirting is a way of communicating your affection for someone and can be
done silently through body language signs, verbally, and by touch. If you
want to keep a girl interested in you, you need to show her even beyond the
flirting game during the first encounter. Let's see what some of the basics of
flirting as a Sigma male are.

Eyes Can Say a Lot

You must have heard the saying "The eyes are windows to your soul" – it's been repeated so many times that it has become a cliché, and you probably remember what we said about creating clichés – cliché is, after all, a universal truth that has been repeated so many times that it has become a part of collective memory. Well, eyes do say a lot, even though they can't say everything there is about you. In the first place, your eyes can reveal your intention.

When flirting with a girl, make sure to maintain eye contact to show that you are listening and that she has your full attention. Likewise, when you are talking to a girl, keep eye contact to let her know that you are honest and confident with your words. Eyes can say a lot, even when no words have been exchanged – remember the body language cues about eyes and how people observe their surroundings.

Good Manners

As a Sigma, you are a true gentleman when it comes to good manners. You respect others regardless of differences, and you respect other people's opinions. Show the girl you like that you respect her and care about her opinion and what she has to say. Listening to her is also a great deal, as you will also show that you are a good listener aside from having good manners to open the doors for a lady or to offer her a seat. We all appreciate respectful behavior, so good manners can take you a long way with a girl.

A Few Words May Take You a Long Way

Sigmas don't rely on small talk and chitchatting that leads nowhere – these social cues just don't make sense to a Sigma who would rather talk about significant topics with a purpose and a goal. Sigma also doesn't share every part of their cognitive process, which means that you may share a conclusion or a philosophy in the form of a fact without explaining the process of how

CHAPTER 5: MAINTAINING INTEREST

you analyze these topics. This may be difficult when flirting, as people mostly rely on small talk to engage in a conversation. However, the girl you like may appreciate how direct you are and how you can say a lot with only a few words.

Don't Crave for Attention

Attention seeking is just not part of Sigma's lifestyle. Sigma doesn't need validation or gratification in the form of being praised by others. He is perfectly aware of himself and all the intricacies that make the person he is. As a true Sigma, you are content with the affection you receive from the people you like, but you are perfectly fine without it as you are more dependent on self-validation. Show the girl you like that you appreciate her interest and attention, but don't act desperate to get it. Instead, rely on your values and everything you appreciate about yourself - if she appreciates your values as well, you will get the attention you need. So, essentially, the key is always appreciating yourself and the things about yourself that make you confident.

Physical Touch

Physical touch is crucial in relationships, and just like body language cues, it can tell a lot about someone's intentions and can equally reveal your affection without the need to word it. Touch her hand with yours, lean on her when you are standing next to each other, and touch her hair occasionally when the situation calls for it. Physical touch makes a relationship stronger and can also make two people grow close to each other.

KEEPING THE GIRL YOU LIKE

Once you get past the period of flirting and courting, in case you want to be in a relationship, there are some things to note, as Sigmas don't usually comply with standard expectations that people have in a relationship. Even though you may have started a relationship, it may be difficult to keep your significant other because Sigmas are not ready to change their lifestyle for anyone – they are independent, self-sufficient, and can go on without socializing for long periods without feeling the need to be around people. When you consider all the personality traits of a Sigma male, it is hard to even imagine that a girl would agree to be in such a relationship where she isn't the priority and where you value the time you spend alone more than you value spending time with someone else.

Another option is to date a girl who shares a similar lifestyle and understands your needs concerning personal space, alone time, and the never-ending need to grow.

Another thing to note about being a Sigma or categorizing yourself as any type in the socio-sexual hierarchy of dominance is that the way these personalities are described is fractal, which means that not all Sigmas are the same. Sigma males may also find joy in sharing their time with someone completely different from them. You can make a significant connection with other people if their company suits you, and if you want to make more time in your day for someone you care about, you will take the initiative as a true Sigma and do it because you want.

Share a Glimpse into Your Mindset

When in a relationship or dating, it is recommended to share some of your thoughts on life and how you see the world. Allow your partner to have a glimpse into your mindset and learn something about how your mind functions. You don't need to spill everything and describe your lifestyle in one go – you can share a glimpse into your mindset in a more natural way and gradually as you spend more time with your partner.

If she is worried when she sees you glancing in the distance, not knowing that you are drifting away with your thoughts, allow her to experience the world from your perspective and briefly explain that this is who you are and that this state is not negative. She might be glad to know that you can be yourself in her presence.

Don't assume that everyone knows the way you function, and this is a logical method of functioning - Sigmas have a more unique lifestyle when compared to Alpha's and Beta's for instance, in the sense that Sigma's lifestyle is perceived as unusual.

Treat Her Right

Even though you are mostly focused on your personal growth and self-improvement, always looking for new experiences, if you want to share a significant relationship with someone, you need to invest in your time with them, too. Spend time with your partner doing something you both enjoy or that she enjoys - trying out new things is important for you, and it is also important for the development and growth of the relationship itself. Treating her right means you are also honest with her as a true Sigma always is, and it also means that you care about her feelings.

If you care about how your partner feels, make sure to share your insights with her and observe her emotional expressions, so you'll know how to treat her accordingly. When you decide to be with someone, even if you don't know where this is leading, give them the best of yourself just like you would do with anything else in life.

Respecting Others

Mutual respect is a necessity. One of the signs that a relationship is working is having both partners respect each other's boundaries, lifestyles, and differences. Respecting someone means that you value them for who they are and that they value you back – this is exactly what you want in a relationship. You don't want to spend your time with someone who can't appreciate you for being yourself, pressuring you into becoming someone else. All the changes you make about yourself need to be made because you want to change and not because someone is emotionally manipulating you into changing. The same goes for your end – you can't force people to change, and as a true Sigma, you are less likely to even want that.

By respecting your partner and receiving respect in the same way, it will also be easier for both of you to express yourself, while you will also feel safe in each other's presence.

Alone But Together

The fact that you like being alone and having time for yourself doesn't mean that you should neglect your partner's needs if your partner knows how to nurture your need for solitude. Even though you like to solve your problems alone, don't be afraid to share them with your partner – your partner will be glad to know that you trust them enough to share your problems with them. They will offer their help, even though they know that you won't take it – don't lecture them about how you like to do things by yourself; instead, thank your partner for being considerate and let them know politely that you don't need their help. That way, you are alone but not apart from your partner as you have just shared something important.

It is also important for a couple to grow and develop together in a relationship, as well as have an individual path of growth and improvement, so make sure to work on your relationship as much as you would work on yourself if you want it to last.

Listen

As we already know, listening is one of the traits that Sigmas have, as they are very insightful and great listeners while they tend to be direct in conversations, cutting straight to the point. Listening to your partner will help you understand their needs and perception of your relationship with them. Luckily, you are a good listener. Still, listening needs to be paired with verbal communication as well. Your partner needs to listen to you and understand your needs, too. Otherwise, the relationship won't work with a one-way effort.

Participate

Do something together and find time for some alone time, not with yourself but with your partner. Both partners need to participate for the relationship to work, which means that you should both be working for a mutual interest – to be happy and content with life in general.

As a mysterious Sigma male, which might have attracted your partner in the first place, you are better at "show" than "tell," so instead of revealing to your partner that you have mastered all your guitar lessons, play her a song after dinner or when you feel like it. Learn her favorite song or surprise her with your tune. Likewise, if you are great at cooking, you are less likely to reveal that to your partner verbally, but you can make her an amazing meal and surprise her instead. This way, you will also spice up your relationship with mystery and awe.

SEX AND SEXUALITY

If it weren't for the sex part, you and your partner might as well be just friends, and that is a fact. Sex is one of the most important aspects of a romantic relationship and is also one of the main reasons why people break up and drift apart. As such, you need to treat sex not only as an enjoyable action or experience but a way to connect with your partner. Sex and the intimacy involved can help you establish and strengthen the emotional connection you have with your partner and strengthen the bond you have with your own body. Sex allows you to explore not only your sexuality but also your and your partner's body in a pleasurable way.

In a way, sex includes many of the things we've been going through in some of the previous chapters of our Sigma guide, as sex can help you boost your confidence, have a meaningful connection with another person, relieve stress, improve your health, and even serve the purpose of a light workout. So, aside from being one of the most enjoyable things for humans, sex can make you feel better, physically and mentally.

Here are some tips on sex and sexuality when it comes to how Sigmas usually explore their sexual interests when in a relationship.

Share Your Interests

One of our tips for keeping a girl you like interested in you was to share your interests and thoughts with her, as communicating with your partner is essential for every healthy relationship. We encourage you to do the same when it comes to sex. Yes, it is not very sexy to have an entire conversation about what you and your partner like in bed, but you can show it to each other instead and make it into a sex game, where each one of you will casually show their partner where they want to be touched or kissed. The most important thing, in this case, is that both of you are comfortable with each other's interests in bed. This is where respect must be included, as you need to respect the boundaries your partner sets, and this respect needs to be mutual.

If you feel comfortable with that, you can also verbally communicate about what you like and don't like, spicing it up with some of that Sigma mystery you have.

Be Kind and Patient

Kindness and patience are some of the most cherished and rarest of human qualities. Being kind to other people shows that you are concerned and generous without the need for validation, which is also an important aspect of every relationship – to understand and appreciate your partner without expecting anything in return. However, there needs to be feedback for the relationship to be healthy, which means that your partner also needs to be kind and patient with you. Patience is not a stranger to assertive Sigmas who know how to approach and handle their problems, while you will also need to be patient with your partner like you are with other things in your life. Have patience and understanding when your partner is feeling well, or when she may have troubles understanding your lifestyle or your need to be alone with your thoughts. You should also expect patience in return, as it must go both ways to keep your connection alive.

Enjoy the Moment

Even the most seemingly stable relationships can collapse and do collapse, which doesn't mean that the relationship was all bad and wrong. Imagine being with someone for years, let's say three years; you've come to know each other rather well, you share so many experiences and can tell how the other is feeling just by the look of them – you have a connection. After a while, you both or one of you feel that you no longer work together for some reason. Even though the relationship ended, there were certainly many great moments during your three years together. It is all these great moments that made your relationship the way it was in the first place. That is why you should enjoy every moment regardless of what the future may bring. This is where your ability to be present can come as more than handy, as you will create an intense and dynamic experience.

Keeping it Fresh and Exciting

To make the relationship long-lasting and as equally dynamic as at the beginning when you were only dating, try keeping the relationship fresh and exciting. The best part is that you don't even have to try that hard to make it happen, and as a huge plus, you will also create great moments to remember. Keeping the relationship exciting also increases the probability of staying together and will even make you more connected with your partner, as you will create these moments together.

Do something together that none of you have ever done before or go on a weekend getaway together. You can try going out to new places and trying out new restaurants in town if that's your thing. Even if it is not, give it a go, at least for a new experience. Touch her when you feel like it to show her your affection. Touch is important for all humans, as it provides us with the feeling of safety, love, affection, and care that we need to thrive. Spending time by yourself is also a great strategy for keeping the relationship fresh, convenient for a Sigma male who appreciates selective solitude. By being apart for a couple of days, you allow each other to grow individually and focus on themselves. You can use that time to meet up with friends, family or to work on yourself.

6

CHAPTER 6: HOW TO STRENGTHEN YOUR SIGMA MALE PERSONALITY

The hierarchical division constructed by Vox Day describes Sigma males as the rarest among men. Sigma could easily become an Alpha as he shares many of the same qualities noted in a leader, but he chooses not to conform. Sigma refuses to be a part of the socio-sexual hierarchy and thus, he can be whatever he wants without feeling the pressure to comply with social norms and hierarchical dominance. As such, these types represent the typical characteristics of different kinds of men that could be categorized as Sigma, Alpha, Beta, Gamma, and Omega but represent only fractal characteristics that could be further classified not only as types but also as stereotypes.

As a Sigma male, you may also have some characteristics noted in any of the listed types as well as those of an Alpha, but it is your conduct that determines who you are as a person. We all have layers, which is why it isn't easy to match a single stereotypical personality. As a true Sigma, you live your life the way you want to and rely on your strengths and work on your weaknesses, all while defying social constructs, so regardless of the hierarchical type that you are "assigned," you are who you want to be.

The most important thing is to keep working on yourself and be aware that self-improvement is a never-ending challenge.

WORKING ON SELF-IMPROVEMENT

Improve yourself in any way you believe is useful for your personality development. Practice self-acceptance, self-love, and self-confidence with any chance you get and become a better person, first and foremost for your own sake.

Here are some of the top tips on maintaining your strength, keeping your body fit, and understanding your needs, emotions, and lifestyle as a Sigma male.

Maintaining Your Mental Strength

You've already started to practice your mental strength, and you have probably come a long way since you've started with this guide. However, just as you need to work on strengthening your resilience and practicing mental strength, you also need to learn how to maintain your fortitude.

- Act like a person you want to become – don't wait to be happy and confident in yourself until you achieve all your goals. Instead, act like the person you want to become and embrace the idea of your better self. This way, you will be setting yourself up for success, instead of being happy after you learn that new skill or after you get promoted, embrace the excitement of working on your goals. You will be happy and content with yourself even before you reach your goals.
- What are you grateful for? Complaining and waiting for a better time to come when you will finally be at peace with yourself and be happy is more difficult than analyzing your achievements and being grateful for what you already achieved. Numerous studies have shown that being grateful and appreciating everything you have in life increases happiness and reduces stress. This way, you can generate more strength to prepare yourself for future achievements.
- Focus on the present – we can't emphasize enough how important it is to embrace mindfulness and just live in the present moment. This

ability will help you through harsh times, as you can always focus on the here-and-now so you can analyze the difficult situation without the pressure and stress caused by the problem.

- Don't give up – never give up on your goals, but make sure your goals are achievable and realistic because you will only grow more misfortunate if you are striving for the impossible. The impossible and possible are defined through your abilities, your motivation, and different circumstances in life. Since you are rather self-aware as a Sigma, you know your limitations and are comfortable with your potential. Motivate yourself into achieving everything you know you can achieve in life.

- Do things that you like – whether you enjoy listening to music, writing, working out, or you have a hobby that you particularly enjoy, just do it. By doing the things we like and enjoy the most, we allow ourselves to thrive and heal when we are down and not feeling well. Enjoying your favorite activities will also have beneficial effects on your body and mind.

- Be in touch with reality – be aware of your problems and the things you need to handle, so you don't fall into a dark pit of delusions, but don't obsess with your problems. Obsessing over things you need to do or the problems you need to handle won't offer any solution and will make you feel depressed and uncomfortable about your place in the world. Instead, think about everything you can do in a day to make you closer to the resolution.

Maintaining Your Physical Appearance

Working out and keeping a healthy diet in check will not only make you fit and healthy but will also make you feel great about yourself, mentally and physically. Physical appearance also sends a message to other people – it discovers how well you are taking care of yourself, how invested you are in self-care, your lifestyle, and your overall conduct.

- Keep up working out – find the workout routine that suits you the best and spend at least half an hour each day swimming, running, jogging, or working out at a local gym. You can keep your weights by your bedside to motivate you to work out in the morning as part of your routine at the start of every new day. Remember, working out doesn't only help us look good but also encourages the production of serotonin and dopamine.

- Take care of your hair and beard – decide on your hairstyle and the style of your beard, which could be no beard as well – and make sure to regularly visit your favorite barbershop. You can also experiment with your look if you feel like it. A nicely groomed beard and hair will also add more points to your confidence.
- Buy new clothes – throw out anything you don't plan to use and don't need, including clothes you no longer see yourself in. Buy some new clothes and combine them with your favorite clothes to create new outfits that you will wear with confidence. Changing something about your style will make you feel brand-new and can be a rather refreshing experience.
- Personal hygiene – a true gentleman takes care of his hygiene, including regular showers, washing your hair, taking care of your skin (skin is the biggest human organ, so take great care of it!), brushing your teeth, and overall staying fresh and clean. Be clean and always feel fresh!

Understanding Your Needs and Emotions

From keeping your physical appearance to keeping your emotions in check, you can't be completely content and happy about yourself if you neglect your emotions and your needs. So focus on what you need, day to day, to stay in touch with yourself – analyze your emotional state whenever you feel like you are losing grasp over how happy you are about your life.

- Understand the origin of your emotions – why do you feel sad or listless today? Why do you feel angry or let down? Whenever you feel a negative emotion crippling upon you, identify it and deal with it at its root before it starts affecting your day, week, month, and life in general. Can you resolve the problem that is causing you to feel bad about yourself? If the answer is "not all at once" or "not at the moment," then you should try practicing being present in the moment and gradually deal with the problem you have. You shouldn't stress about the things you can't change, as this sentiment will only make you feel insecure and weak.

- Listing your needs – you should create a list of what you want and need in life, along with a brief strategy on how to get what you need. Start by asking questions like "What would make me proud of myself?", "What would make me feel secure and safe?", "How can I be happy with myself?" and similar questions that will help you reveal what is it that you lack in life to achieve your goals.

- Emotional connection with other people – even though you are rather self-sufficient as a Sigma, you still need to have a significant emotional bond with at least one person, or you will at least need it at some point in your life. Every human has a universal need to be loved, which is achieved through establishing emotional connections and bonds with other people. To put your self-sufficiency and independence on the side, a significant other can complement your life and make you even more motivated to achieve your goals.

- A sense of achievement – having a sense that you have achieved something complements your mental strength and makes you more confident in yourself. To have a sense of achievement, set smaller goals to achieve each day or every week, even when you are far from completing a goal – that way, you will have a sense of achievement and become more motivated by tracking the gradual process of achieving your goals.

- Self-awareness – as a Sigma, you are self-aware and in touch with your negative and positive traits, so you know what needs to be improved and which traits should be nurtured as they are. This also means that you are aware of how other people perceive you. In addition, you can analyze your emotions and needs with a logical approach. Be in touch with yourself on your best and worst days as you are still you even when things are not working in your favor.

Always Seek for Improvement

It is the very core of Sigma's lifestyle to thrive and strive for better and more. Your ability to perceive yourself through the prism of logic and reality allows you to see yourself as you are, with good things and the bad. That also means you are in constant pursuit of improvement. A Sigma works every day to be a better man for himself the next day, which is how he can be happy even on a difficult journey of self-improvement. The very fact that you are giving your best and working on becoming the best version of yourself should make you happy and at peace, while striving also makes up a more dynamic life where you are challenged to achieve your goals.

Always seek improvement, even in little things, as practice makes everything better, even if you are only taking small steps. It is the journey that counts, not just the final destination. Appreciate your efforts and acknowledge them with self-acceptance and the motivation needed to make good things happen in life. As long as you are working on improving yourself, you have at least a sense that you control your life and your happiness.

Seize the Day

Every day is a new opportunity and a new challenge. If you feel like you achieved nothing today, remember that you always have tomorrow. Every new tomorrow is a brand-new chance for you to try again and remind yourself why you are not giving up on your dreams. Seize the day and get the most out of what you are given in life. Concerning things that you are not given and wish to achieve in life, you can always think through ways to create your opportunities, which is where your mental strength, resilience, and the will to improve will shine.

The day is yours, Sigma, and so is every tomorrow – what you do with your day is what counts in the end.

Made in United States
Orlando, FL
03 October 2023

37518261R00059